WHY WRITE?
WHY READ?

MICHAEL ROSEN

Introduction

As some people reading this may know, I have a blog:

MichaelRosenblog.blogspot.com

where I post up occasional pieces about writing, reading and performing along with my poems and other thoughts.

I have gathered some of my thoughts about reading and response (and how to assess it) in the booklet *Poetry and stories for Primary and Lower Secondary Schools*.

In this booklet I've brought together some of my writing about writing! Unlike a book, the pieces do not develop an argument, nor are they linked in some special way. This is because they are 'occasional' and can be taken as stand-alone, though of course they are all on a theme. I feel that given we are all so busy, and constrained by the curriculum, then distributing these ideas as stand-alone articles in booklets, makes them easier to read.

Please feel free to use these pieces however you want. Some of them may work as discussion points for staff meetings, school clusters, conferences or however you like.

Part 1

The full 'meaning' of a word is not its 'definition'

It's easy to reduce 'meaning' to 'definition'. This leaves out 'connotation': the web of connections a word/phrase/whole text has with our experience. This is yet another way in which 'grammar' (sometimes employed by critics) does not explain all!

The words 'pain au chocolat' and 'chocolatine' mean the 'same'. But they 'connote' different meanings via my, your and our experience.

Ironically, some of the most reductive, most non-connotive approaches to language occur when education and exams approach the most connotive uses of language: literature!

Given that a good deal of poetry works through and with such processes we call 'allusion', 'affect', 'ambiguity', 'resonance', 'evocation', and 'suggestion' – again, how ironic that we keep trying to reduce words or phrases in poems to single meanings or definitions.

Part 2

How 'knowledge about language' for schools could be so much better

If you think of language as a whole, then 'knowledge about language' is made up of anything and everything that describes language or can explain why and how we use it in the ways that we do.

Over the last few years, 'knowledge about language' in the hands of the government, the Department for Education (DfE) and Michael Gove has been reduced to 'grammar' and 'grammar' has been reduced to one model, one form of what 'grammar' might be – a so-called 'structure and function' model.

This single model of 'grammar' (treated as if it's the only model) and enforced through the Grammar, Punctuation and Spelling test, then holds sway over primary education, and primary aged children.

First, to be clear, there are other models of grammar, which, say, treat that word 'function', not as how words 'function' inside sentences (e.g., this noun is the subject of the sentence) but as social functions (e.g., why have so many of us started saying 'So . . . ' at the beginning of our utterances).

For some reason, this form of grammar was not the one implemented and enforced.

There is, though, an even more important criticism to make. 'Knowledge about language' is a massive subject and can't be reduced to 'grammar' of any kind. Since the time of Aristotle, linguists have tried to examine language, describe it and explain it. Aristotle was particularly interested in the 'effects' of particular uses of language and did a damned good job of it. We all know, for example, what 'catharsis' is, thanks to him, but he did more than that in his book *Poetics*.

Over the last 150 years, a huge amount of work has gone into examining how the many different uses of language work and have created disciplines such as narratology, stylistics, pragmatics and intertextuality. Though these are mostly written about in very academic ways, they can be broken down into very accessible (and enjoyable) ways for children and school students to use. To be clear: these are also 'knowledge about language', and because they are tied very closely to 'language in specific uses' and not 'abstract ideals', they are especially useful in helping children speak and write.

Narratology, for example, enables us to examine how stories (or any kind of writing) are 'told': e.g., who narrates? how does the narration change? what kind of narrator is narrating? what devices does the narrator use to 'talk' to us?

Narratology can help us look at how the narration enables us to know how characters think. There are several very different devices that have grown up, all the way from 'she thought' to the 'free indirect discourse' favoured by Jane Austen and many writers of children's books.

Narratology can help us look at 'foregrounding' and 'point of view' – how these shift, favouring one or more characters and why?

Narratology is very useful at helping us with time frames which often change via flashback, flash forward and invocations of continuous time or continuous existence.

Stylistics can take us into how texts 'sound' (prosody) – showing us how repetition of structure and letter sounds make rhythms in texts.

Stylistics can draw attention to sentence length, sentence complexity or simplicity, how paragraphs are constructed across texts, why and how these change as the need to express different things change.

Stylistics can draw attention to 'register' – how informal/formal a text is? How much does it draw on modes of text from which sources – does the writing empty speech modes? Are there deliberate attempts to 'borrow' language from specific sources e.g., from a field different from the one in the text, e.g., from science in a novel?

Stylistics can draw attention to which class of words are repeated e.g., many adjectives, many adverbs – or none?

Pragmatics can draw attention to how dialogue is structured and where the narrator dialogues with the audience/readership. Dialogue can be structured in many different ways in fiction and pragmatics can help us make distinctions.

Intertextuality can help us with the matter of 'borrowing' that I mentioned earlier. In essence, all writing is borrowing in that it borrows the sounds, structures and meanings that have gone before in order to do whatever it does. However, some borrowings are more obvious than others and/or more significant. This can be at the level of a whole genre e.g., *Hamlet* as 'revenge tragedy' or at the level say of using literary motifs or tropes e.g., 'the pathetic fallacy'. Or again allusion to writing or speech that comes before (as Dickens does in the opening pages of *A Christmas Carol*) and so on.

If the government and the DfE had been really interested in a holistic view of language and 'knowledge about language' it would have talked to applied linguists about all this, and then got hold of people who know about pedagogy and asked them to produce materials which applied this 'knowledge about language' in age-appropriate ways, using imitation, and practice and investigation as much as description and direct instruction, so that this 'knowledge about language' could have been applied directly to helping children write well.

But they didn't.

The main reason why they didn't is because the Bew Report of 2011 imposed the SPaG test instead. This was because Michael Gove told them to.

Part 3

Bad Grammar

In the previous section, I said how the disciplines of narratology, stylistics, pragmatics and intertextuality could be used as part of a broad strategy called 'knowledge about language'. My argument is that 'grammar' (as defined by the testing and exam system) has become the tail wagging the dog on this matter and that there are political reasons for why 'grammar' (and this particular kind of grammar) was singled out and blown up into the one key kind of 'knowledge about language' that is being taught in schools. In the next section, I'm going to give you a break down of how those topics, narratology, stylistics, pragmatics and intertextuality can be broken down into very usable 'triggers' for teachers to use in classrooms to help analyse texts, and discover how writing works and to what end. 'Grammar' will be included in this but as only one part.

As I've said before, the particular kind of 'grammar' primary children do, was introduced because Michael Gove inserted it into the Bew Report, which we should remember was not a report on language in the curriculum, but a report on 'Assessment and Accountability'. Grammar, it was stated, has right and wrong answers, and so would be suitable for use as a means to assess and evaluate teachers and teaching. It was not introduced because a combination of linguists, applied linguists, educationists and teachers thought it would be a good idea. It was introduced purely and only because Michael Gove thought that it would be a good way to assess teachers. However, the actual nature of the grammar involved was plucked from a repertoire of 'grammars' and linguistic knowledge that can be taught. It seems to have been based on Gove's reading of Simon Heffer's book(s) on the matter. Simon Heffer is not a linguist. He's a journalist. I reviewed his first book on grammar for BBC Radio 3 and it included several mistakes.

The meat of the issue is that for these political reasons, this kind of grammar and an implied teaching practice to fit the test came into being. The grammar itself is problematic because it is based entirely on a self-sealed system which they call 'structure and function'. The function in question is the function within the sentence or passage of writing, not the function in social use. The argument here is that such grammarians believe that they can divine grammatical systems without explaining any particular system according to why such structures have evolved and why they are used. So, they segment ('chop up') language into the sections they think are valid e.g., words, phrases, main clauses, subordinate clauses etc., and they give them functions e.g., 'subject', or that they 'qualify' or 'modify' other words or phrases or clauses, and so on. Quite why the language is segmented this way is treated as self-evident (the clever grammarians just know it and tell us), and we have to take the internal logic of e.g., 'subject-verb agreement' as again, apparent.

To take this as an example, in fact, in use, the subject-verb agreements they say are 'correct', and which teachers have to teach, and children are tested on, turn out to be not correct for millions of people, who say such things as 'we was', 'I were'. Millions of people are, according to this way of looking at language, wrong. To be clear, they are only wrong, if it has been pre-decided that 'we were' and 'I was' are the only 'correct' forms according to a 'rule' invented by grammarians called 'subject-verb agreement' and that there can only be one form of 'agreement', the one we say is right. Why can't we live with variation? Some people say one thing, others say another. After all, we tolerate variation in many other parts of language use. In fact, what happened was that grammarians drew up 'conjugations' of verbs based on what they said was 'one correct form', and claimed that this represented some 'real' category called the 'singular' and 'plural' form of the verb ('was' and 'were' when used in the 'first person' ('I' or 'we') even though millions were using it in different ways! Hundreds of years later, thousands of children sit down in a test that is used to assess teachers, and have to spot the 'right' 'subject-verb' agreement! We are not talking about scientific descriptions here. We are talking about a false categorisation foisted on to teachers and pupils.

Because none of this is connected directly to use and social purpose, the whole field is full of arguments and disputes about terminology and whether bits of the language really 'are' such-and-such or not. Teachers will be very familiar with the argument about 'connectives', 'conjunctions' and 'adverbs' where they were, in essence, victims of two or three very dogmatic schools of thought claiming that such-and-such a word really 'is' a connective or really is a conjunction or, in another example, really is an adverb. Similar arguments break out over the categories of words e.g., over 'infinitives', 'subjunctives' or 'determiners' and it's often hard to work out whether the name for one kind of word, e.g., a 'modal verb' is a sub-category of another, in this case, it's clearly a sub-class of 'verb', but is it a sub-class of 'auxiliary' verb or a parallel class? Looking across the English-speaking world, or across time (e.g., in my lifetime) there are variations between those who would describe 'my' in 'my hat' as a 'possessive determiner' while others call it a 'possessive adjective'.

If you follow any of this closely, you might be interested in this: for all my life studying English, learning French, German and Latin, I've been used to hearing the term 'tense' to describe one feature of verbs. We're all used to throwing around 'past', 'present' and 'future' and where necessary attaching the word 'continuous' when '-ing' endings are used. Slightly more complicated: the words 'perfect', 'imperfect' or 'pluperfect' might be used. Again, the terminology-lovers get 'essentialist' about it and say, that such-and-such a verb 'is' the 'present' or 'is' the 'perfect' or whatever. Because all this is a sealed system, not attached to real-life social use, this way of describing verbs gets reduced in the exercises and tests in such a way, that writing, let's say, 'I walk in', gets reduced to saying this 'is' the 'present'. What's wrong with saying that? Well, you don't know that this really 'in the present' until you hear it in the context in which it's spoken. Most of us, at some or another tell stories, or give accounts of events in the past by using the so-called 'present' form of the verb. (This sometimes gets called the 'historic present' to cover it.) 'I walk in' or 'Napoleon gets on his horse' can indeed be part of an account that took place in the past. Meanwhile the form we use in novels to tell stories that are unfolding in the present is the same form we use to recount things that happened in the past: 'Harry Potter wore glasses' means in the book, that in the present of the book, Harry Potter 'is' wearing glasses. In some countries, novels are told using what has been called the 'present' form of the verb. People having the unfortunate task of teaching 'grammar' to 10 and 11 year olds have to explain that 'I have eaten' is now called the 'present perfect' because, according to the people who invented this term, whatever happened is connected to the present. Most people might reasonably think that if they say, 'I have eaten', the matter of eating is now closed. It happened. It's finished. There's nothing 'present' about it. So what's going on here?

Such 'grammarians' have spotted that 'have' is a 'present' form of the verb so 'I have eaten', they say, must have something of the 'present' in it! This is an example of treating language as a sealed system, with terminology cooked up to justify or slot in with previous terminologies and not with actual social use. Having learned that it's the 'present perfect' in Year 6, students go into Year 7 and 8, learn French, and hear that 'I have eaten/J'ai mangé' is the 'passé compose' (meaning literally, the 'composed past') or just the 'perfect'. But surely the 'future tense' is a fixed matter? Not so, say some, because where in French the 'future' is created by doing something with the end of the verb, in English we use the word 'will', so it's not a 'tense' as such, say some, it's just a use of an auxiliary. But hang on, we have another way of doing it: using 'going to'. So is 'going to go' a 'future' tense or not?

But hang on again, we can use the 'present' to indicate futurity. 'What are you doing tomorrow?' 'I'm going out.' Clearly this conversation is all about the future, but has used the 'present' in order to tell it. Well, in truth it's not the 'present' in the present, then is it?

Some other grammarians have stepped into this world of 'tenses' and have announced that the term 'tense' is so problematic, we should dispense with it, and think instead of 'aspect'. This, they say, would dispense with linking a particular form of the verb to a particular time frame (e.g., 'I go' is 'present') but always look at the particular use and describe that.

Now all this kind of argument is kept well away from teachers and pupils. That's because we're talking here about the equivalent of magic. They believe that it's vital for this stuff to be taught and learned as something fixed by incredibly clever, experienced people who know all about this code that lies behind and beyond language. If you suggest that all this terminology is much debated, is wobbly, fuzzy, and indeed provisional, then it can't be imposed as the right/wrong system required by the Bew Report in order to assess teachers. Then again, if the whole system has problems (because it's self-referential and doesn't connect directly with use) then the whole edifice of diktat and authority is undermined. It must not happen.

And you shouldn't have read this.

Unread it immediately.

The worst aspect of all this, though, is that the grammar in question is then used to produce 'writing at the expected level'. Arbitrary categories such as 'fronted adverbials', 'expanded noun phrases' and 'embedded relative clauses' and 'complex sentences' are used as criteria for what makes 'good' writing. Teachers are forced to tell children that because they are using fronted adverbials, expanding their noun phrases and embedding their relative clauses, they are writing well.

As I hope to show in the next chapter, 'technical' descriptions of language can involve a wide array of methods. These don't claim to be 'rules' but are tailored to language in use and language in use is of course incredibly diverse and uses 'variants'. Some of these methods may be useful in helping children and students to write. Given that writing is a very complex matter, it's foolish to make great claims for any one method which will itself, on its own, definitely deliver up good writing. People in government and people who devise assessment systems have to say such nonsense.

PS, I know I've told this story before, but enjoy it if you haven't. Last year, Schools Minister Nick Gibb was asked on to the BBC Radio 4, World at One programme to talk about the grammar test for Year 6 (10 and 11 year olds). He explained how important it is, because he's slotted it into his world view that 'knowledge' is 'knowledge' and that more knowledge is good, less knowledge is bad, and even though the testing system he so loves, segregates children precisely on the basis of whether they have more or less knowledge, he keeps telling himself that the kids are getting cleverer now, thanks to the Tories.

So the news programme's presenter, Martha Kearney read Nick a sentence and asked him if a given word in a sentence that she read to him was a 'subordinate conjunction' or a 'preposition'. Poor Nick. He struggled and then said the 'wrong' thing. Before we laugh at his misfortune, though, ask the question, in the example that Martha gave, was the distinction between two categories ('subordinate conjunction' and 'preposition') really valid? (The actual example doesn't matter!) Oh yes, say some grammarians. Oh no, say some others! So poor old Nick struggled to get 'right' something that the grammar test asks for, but which may not be right OR wrong anyway!!! Remember what Lord Bew said in the grammar test? Grammar can be used to assess teachers because it has right/wrong answers. No, Lord Bew, it's you who can be deemed right or wrong on this matter, and in this case, you were wrong, as evidenced by Nick Gibb, who is still smarting under the indignity of Martha Kearney telling him that he was 'wrong'. In reality, it was the question that Martha plucked from the GPS paper that was wrong, not Nick Gibb, and not any of thousands of children and teachers who were told that they had got it 'wrong' too.

PPS, the dispute in question is over the use of the words 'after', 'before' or 'since' in sentences like (1) 'He went to the loo, after the concert' and (2) 'He went to the loo, after the concert was over'. One school says that the first 'after' in (1) is a 'preposition' and the second (2) is a 'subordinate conjunction'. Another school says that the distinction – in this circumstance – is invalid.

Part 4

Using narratology, stylistics, pragmatics, intertextuality in analysing passages of writing

In this section, I want to break down the topics or disciplines of narratology, stylistics, pragmatics and intertextuality into triggers which we can use productively as ways of examining how texts work. If we link this to ideology we might get a view on why these methods were used by any given writer.

Note: these triggers or categories are not meant to be watertight; they can be adapted, and recycled to use or merge with other triggers.

Note 2 – I am of course aware that thousands of English teachers have used some or all of these categories before and indeed used many others. However, some (many?) have not. I am offering this because they've proven useful to me in the past, and also to some of my students. I am not making great claims for being original here. I fully understand that I might be re-inventing the wheel on some, most or all of them.

1. How is the text narrated? Why is it being narrated this way? Categories here might be e.g., 'omniscient narrator' 'multiple narrators', 'unreliable narrator', 'first person narrator' 'self-conscious narrator' (who reveals that he/she/it is narrating). At any given moment and at all moments, a text is narrated. The question here is how and why? John Stephens (academic) argues that how a text is narrated is very 'ideological'. In his analysis, a first person narrative is un-complex and nearly always seeks to make the reader 'identify' with the narrator, be on the narrator's side. Other kinds of narratives can be more complex and ask the reader to take up varying positions and attitudes to different characters and situations. This leads to the reader debating more matters of right and wrong, appropriate and inappropriate etc.

2. Time frames. At any given moment and at all moments a text is in a time frame. It's possible and frequent for texts to move backwards and forwards in time. It's possible for texts to indicate continuous states of being in the past, present or future e.g., 'Rasheda loved movies.' 'Thin' texts stick largely to one time frame. 'Thick' texts, take you backwards and forwards indicating depth, breadth, background, motive etc.

3. Depiction of thought. How does the text indicate what someone is thinking? The most obvious way is 'She thought . . . ' but there are many variations including one in which the text seems to just 'slide' into the protagonist's mind. It's often done with question in the third person: Rasheda finished reading. Now what should she do next?' This kind of writing has a name: 'free indirect discourse'. Texts which choose not to show us people's thoughts (e.g., folk ballads) are different from those that do. (Clearly!)

4. Point of view, foregrounding and focalisation. These slightly different terms point out that any given moment in a text, we are looking at someone or something from a point of view. If it's through the view of a protagonist, we can call that protagonist at that moment the 'focaliser'. This is all very ideological and political. Think gender, race, class, disability etc., and look to see how and which protagonist is focalised or is the focaliser. Why? How?

5. Prosody – this means the musicality of a text and is usually applied to poetry and song lyrics but in fact can be applied to any text, particularly when the text appears to make rhythm and alliteration very apparent. However, it can also be done with sentence length, repetition of words or phrases, or breaks in rhythm and the like.

5a. Sentences – without going particularly into the grammar of sentences – you can tell a lot of what is going on with texts by comparing lengths of sentences. Sometimes writers use a series of short sentences and then a long one. Or there might be a series of long sentences, broken by one single short one. These days, many writers create 'non-grammatical' sentences i.e., they don't 'obey the rule' that a sentence must have a finite verb in it. Dickens did this on the opening page of *Bleak House*. It's very common these days. Why? Some writers use elaborate (over-elaborate?) long sentences with many 'clauses'. Why? Sentences create rhythms, which you can look at when looking at prosody.

6. How are people, settings, creatures, and events evoked or described? This can be done e.g., with incremental material detail. It can be done describing inner states of being. It can be done using figurative language (metaphors and similes). It can be done by the narrator appearing to take a stance towards that setting, creature person or event. Is this sympathetic, hostile, mocking, ironic? If so, why? How is that irony produced? How do we know it's ironic?

7. All texts use other texts from before. In fact, at every level word, phrase, clause, paragraph, chapter, genre – previous texts are borrowed. But borrowings also go on at the level of motif, trope, and rhetorical device. All this is 'intertextuality'. You can play the game of intertextuality-spotting'. What does the text appear to have borrowed? Why? How has the text worked variations on what it has borrowed? (i.e., how has the text 'transformed its sources'? Why?) Rhetorical devices can be found in books of rhetorical devices (!) e.g., an excellent one by Sam Leith. There are also books that include or write up literary motifs and tropes e.g., 'pathetic fallacy' etc.

8. All texts conceal as they reveal. Whenever they intimate that they are going to be saying something later, they can invoke or imply danger, fear, loss, spookiness, uncanniness. They can use time-frame switches to indicate there is more to come. Even phrases like 'once upon a time' are revealing-concealing devices which hook readers/listeners in because they say, I am telling you that this happened 'once upon a time' while everyone listening knows that the phrase means there's more to come but which I haven't told you yet! Reveal-conceal is very important for 'hooking' readers, calling on them to read more and more.

9. Writerliness – this describes how texts refer to the fact they are texts. This is part of self-conscious narration or removal of the 'fourth wall' in films and plays. Narrators can do it, or protagonists can step out of role and appear to talk to the reader/listener/viewer.

10. Register or code. Texts have to use a 'voice' or many voices which precede it. This kind of borrowing is intertextual but can be looked at separately. Particularly interesting, is when, say, narrations switch register, one moment being, say, very formal another appearing to adopt the 'voice' of someone talking. Narrations can borrow the 'voices' (through culturally or professionally specific groups) of trades, classes, localities. Clearly characters do this, but we'll look at that under 'dialogue'.

11. Dialogue – pragmatics. This is a huge subject but of course is crucial for drama, film and novels. I am no way doing this justice here!

It might be useful to compare text dialogue with transcripts of people in real dialogue. The comparison will reveal that text dialogue features much fewer interruptions, hesitations, ellipses, repetitions than real dialogue. How far from 'real' speech is the dialogue? What methods are used to make it seem more like real speech? e.g., through interruption, hesitate, ellipses and repetition? One thing a written text can't do is show directly that people are talking at the same time, and yet we do this in real life!

How is the dialogue narrated? Using simple tags, tags with adverbs? Passages of description between the dialogue? What is being described? People, setting, weather? Inner states of mind and motive?

It might be useful to look at whether the dialogue shows people as developing understandings and co-operating? Or being antagonistic? It might be useful to develop some sub-categories here, e.g., at the level of how dialogue is represented in terms of how are people taking turns?

You might want to look at what is 'revealed/concealed' by the dialogue. Are there unspoken, unstated, implied things being said which the writing wants you to pick up on but the narration doesn't spell out? Alternatively – think Enid Blyton and e.g., 'That served her right' – some texts narrate a commentary on the dialogue that spells things out.

12. All these features can be analysed and/or summated in terms of ideology. This comes from constantly a) finding ways to describe what's going on in any particular category and then b) asking why? Why would the author have written the text this way? And/or what does the text 'imply' even if the author intended it or not? Ideology can taken to be something like the 'message' but if we look at why, say, a book is narrated in a particular way, then ideology becomes more subtle, and more difficult to pin down. Or, take focalisation – what if, like the beginning of *A Christmas Carol* where the narrator is the focaliser for the first page or so? When we look at Dickens's preface to the book, we can see a certain urgency about how he, Charles Dickens, wanted to make a point with this book. He wanted to say, I Charles Dickens have stuff to tell you about the state of Britain. So, we might say, that this need – perhaps egotistical, but also highly political – goes some of the way to explaining why the narration is so strongly self-conscious and insistent in the first pages of the story.

Useful books:

Exploring the Language of Poems, Plays and Prose, Mick Short (Routledge)

Dictionary of Narratology, Gerald Prince (University of Nebraska Press)

Language and Ideology of Children's Fiction, John Stephens (This is the best book I know to make a case for the ideology of narration.)

You Talkin' to me? Rhetoric from Aristotle to Obama, Sam Leith

Narrative Fiction: Contemporary Poetics, Shlomith Rimmon-Kenan

In the next section, I'll try to apply these categories to the opening pages of *A Christmas Carol* and *Emil and the Detectives*.

Part 5

Using literary methods to find out how the opening of *A Christmas Carol* works, and what is it trying to say?

In a previous section, I produced several 'trigger' questions as ways of breaking down the categories of narratology, stylistics, pragmatics, intertextuality and ideology. The list was not intended to be a programme to be adhered to rigidly, nor was it intended to be exhaustive. The categories are not intended to be watertight or distinct from one another. There are overlaps between them and within these categories there are sub-categories. Please don't treat this is as a regime.

I suggested at the end of the list that I would look at the opening pages of Charles Dickens's *A Christmas Carol* and apply these categories.

If you're reading on with this, it may well help if you use some notes as with say, the online 'Sparknotes' or the Penguin Classics edition which has handy footnotes at the back for phrases and terms no longer used, like 'upon 'Change' which was slang for 'at the Royal Exchange'.

Immediately below is an abridged form of the list as a recap.

1. How is the text narrated? Why is it being narrated this way? Categories here might be e.g., 'omniscient narrator' 'multiple narrators', 'unreliable narrator', 'first person narrator' 'self-conscious narrator' (who reveals that he/she/it is narrating). At any given moment and at all moments, a text is narrated. The question here is how and why? [narratology]

2. Time frames. At any given moment and at all moments a text is in a time frame. It's possible and frequent for texts to move backwards and forwards in time. It's possible for texts to indicate continuous states of being in the past, present or future. [narratology]

3. Depiction of thought. How does the text indicate what someone is thinking? [narratology]

4. Point of view, foregrounding and focalisation. These slightly different terms point out that any given moment in a text, we are looking at someone or something from a point of view. [narratology]

5. Prosody – this means the musicality of a text [stylistics]

5a. Sentences – without going particularly into the grammar of sentences – you can tell a lot of what is going on with texts by comparing lengths of sentences. [stylistics]

6. How are people, settings, creatures, and events evoked or described? [stylistics]

7. All texts use other texts from before. In fact, at every level word, phrase, clause, paragraph, chapter, genre – previous texts are borrowed. But borrowings also go on at the level of motif, trope, and rhetorical device. [intertextuality]

8. All texts conceal as they reveal. [narratology]

9. Writerliness – this describes how texts refer to the fact they are texts. [narratology]

10. Register or code. Texts have to use a 'voice' or many voices which precede it. [stylistics]

11. Dialogue

How is the dialogue narrated? Using simple tags, tags with adverbs? Passages of description between the dialogue? What is being described? People, setting, weather? Inner states of mind and motive? [pragmatics]

12. All these features can be analysed and/or summated in terms of ideology. This comes from constantly a) finding ways to describe what's going on in any particular category and then b) asking why? Why would the author have written the text this way? And/or what does the text 'imply' even if the author intended it or not? [ideology]

Here is the text from the opening of A *Christmas Carol*:

A Christmas Carol

PREFACE

I HAVE endeavoured in this Ghostly little book, to raise the Ghost of an Idea, which shall not put my readers out of humour with themselves, with each other, with the season, or with me. May it haunt their houses pleasantly, and no one wish to lay it.

Their faithful Friend and Servant,

C. D.

December, 1841

STAVE I: MARLEY'S GHOST

Marley was dead: to begin with. There is no doubt whatever about that. The register of his burial was signed by the clergyman, the clerk, the undertaker, and the chief mourner. Scrooge signed it. And Scrooge's name was good upon 'Change, for anything he chose to put his hand to.

Old Marley was as dead as a door-nail.

Mind! I don't mean to say that I know, of my own knowledge, what there is particularly dead about a door-nail. I might have been inclined, myself, to regard a coffin-nail as the deadest piece of ironmongery in the trade. But the wisdom of our ancestors is in the simile; and my unhallowed hands shall not disturb it, or the Country's done for. You will therefore permit me to repeat, emphatically, that Marley was as dead as a door-nail.

Scrooge knew he was dead? Of course he did. How could it be otherwise? Scrooge and he were partners for I don't know how many years. Scrooge was his sole executor, his sole administrator, his sole assign, his sole residuary legatee, his sole friend, and sole mourner. And even Scrooge was not so dreadfully cut up by the sad event, but that he was an excellent man of business on the very day of the funeral, and solemnised it with an undoubted bargain. The mention of Marley's funeral brings me back to the point I started from. There is no doubt that Marley was dead. This must be distinctly understood, or nothing wonderful can come of the story I am going to relate. If we were not perfectly convinced that Hamlet's Father died before the play began, there would be nothing more remarkable in his taking a stroll at night, in an easterly wind, upon his own ramparts, than there would be in any other middle-aged gentleman rashly turning out after dark in a breezy spot – say Saint Paul's Churchyard for instance – literally to astonish his son's weak mind.

Scrooge never painted out Old Marley's name. There it stood, years afterwards, above the warehouse door: Scrooge and Marley. The firm was known as Scrooge and Marley. Sometimes people new to the business called Scrooge Scrooge, and sometimes Marley, but he answered to both names. It was all the same to him.

Oh! But he was a tight-fisted hand at the grindstone, Scrooge! a squeezing, wrenching, grasping, scraping, clutching, covetous, old sinner! Hard and sharp as flint, from which no steel had ever struck out generous fire; secret, and self-contained, and solitary as an oyster. The cold within him froze his old features, nipped his pointed nose, shrivelled his cheek, stiffened his gait; made his eyes red, his thin lips blue; and spoke out shrewdly in his grating voice. A frosty rime was on his head, and on his eyebrows, and his wiry chin. He carried his own low temperature always about with him; he iced his office in the dogdays; and didn't thaw it one degree at Christmas.

External heat and cold had little influence on Scrooge. No warmth could warm, no wintry weather chill him. No wind that blew was bitterer than he, no falling snow was more intent upon its purpose, no pelting rain less open to entreaty. Foul weather didn't know where to have him. The heaviest rain, and snow, and hail, and sleet, could boast of the advantage over him in only one respect. They often 'came down' handsomely, and Scrooge never did.

Nobody ever stopped him in the street to say, with gladsome looks, 'My dear Scrooge, how are you? When will you come to see me?' No beggars implored him to bestow a trifle, no children asked him what it was o'clock, no man or woman ever once in all his life inquired the way to such and such a place, of Scrooge. Even the blind men's dogs appeared to know him; and when they saw him coming on, would tug their owners into doorways and up courts; and then would wag their tails as though they said, 'No eye at all is better than an evil eye, dark master!'

But what did Scrooge care! It was the very thing he liked. To edge his way along the crowded paths of life, warning all human sympathy to keep its distance, was what the knowing ones call 'nuts' to Scrooge.

Once upon a time – of all the good days in the year, on Christmas Eve – old Scrooge sat busy in his counting-house. It was cold, bleak, biting weather: foggy withal: and he could hear the people in the court outside, go wheezing up and down, beating their hands upon their breasts, and stamping their feet upon the pavement stones to warm them. The city clocks had only just gone three, but it was quite dark already – it had not been light all day – and candles were flaring in the windows of the neighbouring offices, like ruddy smears upon the palpable brown air. The fog came pouring in at every chink and keyhole, and was so dense without, that although the court was of the narrowest, the houses opposite were mere phantoms. To see the dingy cloud come drooping down, obscuring everything, one might have thought that Nature lived hard by, and was brewing on a large scale.

The door of Scrooge's counting-house was open that he might keep his eye upon his clerk, who in a dismal little cell beyond, a sort of tank, was copying letters. Scrooge had a very small fire, but the clerk's fire was so very much smaller that it looked like one coal. But he couldn't replenish it, for Scrooge kept the coal-box in his own room; and so surely as the clerk came in with the shovel, the master predicted that it would be necessary for them to part. Wherefore the clerk put on his white comforter, and tried to warm himself at the candle; in which effort, not being a man of a strong imagination, he failed.

'A merry Christmas, uncle! God save you!' cried a cheerful voice. It was the voice of Scrooge's nephew, who came upon him so quickly that this was the first intimation he had of his approach.

'Bah!' said Scrooge, 'Humbug!'

He had so heated himself with rapid walking in the fog and frost, this nephew of Scrooge's, that he was all in a glow; his face was ruddy and handsome; his eyes sparkled, and his breath smoked again. 'Christmas a humbug, uncle!' said Scrooge's nephew. 'You don't mean that, I am sure?'

'I do,' said Scrooge. 'Merry Christmas! What right have you to be merry? What reason have you to be merry? You're poor enough.'

1. Narration:

How many narrators are there, and how should we describe them?

a) C.D. who has written the Preface in which C.D. says that he wants to 'raise the Ghost of an Idea'.

b) The voice using 'I' and offering views and thoughts e.g., 'I don't mean to say that I know . . .'

c) The 'omniscient narrator' who narrates the action, Scrooge's thoughts, dialogue and the thoughts of other protagonists.

We shouldn't really take C.D. and 'b' the 'I' in the story itself as exactly the same. In the Preface, C.D. is talking outside of the story about what he intends the story to be and do. Within the story, the narrator is commenting on protagonists who do not exist in real life. They are 'textualised' beings, created out of signifiers. That said, it's intellectually and emotionally possible to treat a) and b) as the same, especially as Dickens was then and still is/was so clearly a person, a story-teller, and actor. However, clearly the 'I' narrator of a) and b) fades away, as the voice goes into the convention of the omniscient narrator. As an indicator of omniscience and literary history, this voice ('c') uses the phrase 'Once upon a time . . .'.

Other observations about this play between types of narration: 'b' argues with itself, and has conversations with itself (or is with the imagined or implied reader?) – 'Mind! I don't mean to say that I know . . .' and 'Scrooge knew he was dead? Of course he did? How could it be otherwise?' and 'You will therefore permit me to repeat . . .'.

What does this do rhetorically? We might perhaps say that because it appears to be having conversations it 'invites the reader in to the story to participate in the telling'. As a voice, it's 'borrowed' from live story-telling, where there is an audience who can respond with facial expressions and words to what the teller asks. But why is Dickens doing this? It breaks the fourth wall of story-writing because it reveals that it is doing telling. In fact, there are several clear indicators of this: 'Marley was dead: to begin with.' To begin what? This means, I take it, 'the story'. It draws attention to itself i.e., meaning: 'I am telling you this story which begins here.' without actually quite saying that. In paragraph 4, this narrator says, 'the story I am going to relate', an explicit self-referential part of story-telling/writing. It admits to the artifice of writing/telling to the reader/listener. But why? Why is it so important for Dickens (the real writer) to put this 'I' in the story and be so insistent about it? Under the category of ideology I'm going to try to answer that.

2. Time-frames

In fiction we can take it that there is at least one past – perhaps several – which can be indicated by verbs such as 'he had done' something, or with words like 'earlier' or 'previously' or 'he remembered the time when'. The present in English writing is (confusingly) usually described with e.g., 'The door of Scrooge's house was open . . .' which in speech we would usually use to describe the 'past'. 'The door was open . . .' usually in speech would describe something that happened earlier than now. The 'present' of a story has a name in narratology, it's the 'diegesis'. It means the time and setting of the story. 'Diagetic' is the adjective to describe this e.g., diagetic action means the action taking place in the 'now' of the story.

In these opening lines we have several time frames!

'Marley was dead' (i.e., he died before the story started).

'to begin with' (i.e., in the time frame of 'me' telling you this story).

'Scrooge's name was good upon 'Change' i.e., a continuous time frame in the past and extending into the 'now' (the diegesis). This time-frame (i.e., the continuous state of Scrooge) carries on for a good part of the opening pages.

Following 'Once upon a time' (a phrase which fixes the diegesis, the 'now', we hear 'old Scrooge sat busy in his counting house'.

This time frame is interrupted by some further continuous past-present descriptions such as 'the clerk's fire was so very much smaller'

In a difficult construction, Dickens interrupts the continuous with 'and so surely as the clerk came in with the shovel, the master predicted that it would be necessary for them to part.' This means, if Bob Cratchit came in with a whole shovel full of coal, Scrooge warned that he would sack him. This is not exactly 'continuous'. It's more one or more incidents that gave rise to consequences.

A slightly different time-frame appears when:

Scrooge's nephew arrived: 'He had so heated himself . . .' i.e., the moment immediately prior to him arriving.

A similar time-switch to the immediate past before the 'now' happened when the text says, 'The city clocks had only just gone three'. Note: not that the clocks stood at three' or 'struck three' but they had happened just a moment earlier. I'm not sure why Dickens would do this, other than to indicate a 'realism', in that clocks striking three bang in the moment of the diegesis suggests a coincidence, where all that's intended here is a sense of time passing, not something significant attached to 'three'. (Just a thought).

However, we spot here, the ease with which such a text can switch between diegesis and several different kinds of past very quickly.

Returning to the part where the 'I' narrator says, 'I am going to relate', we might say that this is at least a reference to the time-frame of the future, even if we don't yet go there! However, it's not the time-frame of the diegesis, (the now of the story), it's a reference to the 'now of the story-telling process!

These time-frames are not just significant in themselves. They are significant in that they are 'switches' and we might ask why and how they are managed. I think they exist in this story because Dickens wanted to tell a 'thick' story, full of reflections to and from between past, present and future, (as exemplified, of course, by the ghosts). This is because he wanted to tell a tale of consequence and change, someone reflecting on differences between his past and present, and the possible route to the future. A 'thin' telling would just be an 'and then . . . and then' type story which doesn't go back or forwards in time from the diegesis, the now. Think of ballads for this as a classic 'thin' narrative style.

The arrival of the diegesis as late as the ninth paragraph suggests to me that Dickens very much wanted to be saying to his audience that he was in control of this narrative. So, though it goes into omniscient narration, we should only think of this as the 'I' and/or Dickens doing this. (That's my theory, anyway!) I'll come back to this under 'ideology'.

3. Depiction of thought

a) one kind of thought we come across straightaway is the thought of the 'I' narrator: 'of my own knowledge . . . I don't know how many years'. This is the first person narration of thought, much loved of modern YA fiction. It is usually taken as being 'reliable' unless, through irony, or events revealed later on, it is shown to be 'unreliable'. It can also be complex when it crosses time-frames as with *Great Expectations* where the older Pip reflects on the actions and thoughts of the younger Pip.

At least one irony emerges in this 'I' narration: the self-interruptions, which 'pretend' as if they just 'happen'. 'The mention of Marley's funeral brings me back to the point I started from'. Well, it was you who mentioned the funeral, not us!, we might say. This is followed by the jokey digression about *Hamlet*. Is the writer Dickens, telling us that this narrator is flawed? Liable to be a bit wordy and easily distracted from the flow of his own telling? I think there's a hint of this. This doesn't make this narrator 'unreliable' but at the very least 'slightly flawed', perhaps. I think there's an intention here to introduce a bit of light-heartedness, at the very least too. Perhaps this ties with an interesting phrase in paragraph two: 'Scrooge and he were partners for I don't know how many years'. What do you mean, narrator, you 'don't know'?! Of course you do, it's you telling the story, you making up the character (he's not real is he?) so if you want to say 'how many years' you could; if you don't want to, you don't have to! In other words, it's pretence that this character, Scrooge, exists, that the narrator 'knows' him but his knowledge about him is limited, though he will do his best to relate all he knows. It's a tiny piece of ironic, self-referential, jokey narration.

I tell the story, that I recite:

33

'Down behind the dustbin
I met a dog called Jim.
He didn't know me
and I didn't know him.'
A boy said to me, 'How do you know his name was Jim then?'
And I said, 'Er . . . I don't know . . . sorry.'

It's the same game, where an author pretends that the incident is real (and not created by the author, and has incomplete knowledge of the person etc.)

b) We hear of Scrooge's thoughts both from the 'I' narrator and the omniscient one: 'Scrooge knew he was dead? Of course he did'. This then is still very much in the control of the 'I' narrator, telling us what he knows, creating the story under our eyes. However, there is a way of describing this as a form of 'free indirect discourse' rather than a conversation the narrator is having with himself. That construction of the question and answer to delineate thought without saying 'he thought' is 'free' of the tag 'he thought', it's indirect as with indirect speech ('I' turns to 'he') and it's part of 'discourse' i.e., the telling of the story. We get another hint of this with ''he answered to both names, it was all the same to him' from paragraph 4. This is Scrooge's continuous thought about how people addressed him. We get it again in paragraph 9: 'But what did Scrooge care? It was the very thing he liked.' This is the technique of giving privileged access to a protagonist's thoughts without telling the reader that this is what you are doing. It was created most clearly for the first time by Jane Austen who wanted us to be privy to the thoughts of her key characters in a seemingly invisible or unobtrusive way. It is one of the tricks of realist writing . . . we arrive in the protagonist's head without it being signalled by words like 'he thought'. Dickens wants us to believe that Scrooge is 'real'. So this free indirect discourse method ties in with the narrator pretending to not know 'how many years', or 'the clock had just struck three'.

c) The omniscient narrator (which I've indicated doesn't start happening (arguably) until after 'Once upon a time' indicates how Scrooge is thinking like this: 'this was the first intimation he had of his approach'. As we'll see when we get to the pragmatics (dialogue) this method of going from outside (action) to inside (thought) can have a delaying effect in writing. This may be useful if you want to construct a joke, or a climax or a surprise. I think that this is what's going on here. As we shall see!

Later in the story, of course, there are many more ways in which the omniscient narrator shows us Scrooge's thoughts. It has to, because the story is in a way, about how Scrooge changes his mind i.e., his thoughts!

4. Point of view

Stories use the process of 'focalisation', they bring protagonists to the fore or put them to the rear. They 'foreground' or 'efface' protagonists. We might ask, for example, why choose your protagonist to be an animal? Or why do we only see one protagonist's p.o.v.? Why do we see, say, sudden shifts in focalisation? Or none? What does this do? Bertolt Brecht much admired Shakespeare because of the way in which we not only hear the words of protagonists but frequently hear how others think of the protagonist. Famously, just before we see Antony in *Antony and Cleopatra* two men are having a conversation about Antony: 'The triple of the world transform'd. Into a strumpet's fool: behold and see.' Conflicting and contrasting points of view enable or encourage readers to debate rights and wrongs and whether people are really who they say they are. 'Thick' narratives encourage a lot of this, 'thin' narratives less so, is one argument about literature.

The focalisation in this part of *A Christmas Carol* shifts from the 'I' narrator, placing himself at the heart of the opening, to and from Scrooge, to (at the end of this passage) the nephew. Arguably, in the *Hamlet* digression there is a little p.o.v. shift to seeing things from the p.o.v. of a hypothetical 'middle aged gentleman' turning up in Saint Paul's Churchyard. And following that, the 'son' who has a 'weak mind'. Perhaps this signals the literariness of this story. It will be, it announces, in the tradition of English Literature: look out for antecedents!

More significantly we have a short foregrounding of 'Nature' who 'lived hardly by, brewing on a large scale'. This flags up perhaps that even though this is a 'Christmas' story, it is also pagan. For a moment we'll see things, the text says, from the p.o.v. of 'Nature' – whoever that is!

Other p.o.v. shifts happen, say in paragraph 8, when we meet 'blindman's dogs' who have thoughts: 'appeared to know him' and focalise action around Scrooge. In this paragraph there is even 'negative focalisation' i.e., what people don't do! 'No beggars implored him to . . .'. The writer conjures up a scene that doesn't happen in order to indicate something of the main protagonist's personality! As we'll see under intertextuality this is a rhetorical device too.

All this tells us that the story is going to be wide-ranging in its choice of p.o.v. that it might do this rapidly, or on occasions intensely, focussing in on one protagonist. This is flexible writing, that keeps the reader shifting focus, again one of the instruments of 'realist' writing in that it invites the reader to think that 'everything' is on display, everything can be 'seen' or 'heard' or 'known about'. It's an illusion, but it's part of the game of 'realism'.

5. and 5a. Prosody and sentences – the musicality of the writing

It's possible to run the prosody meter (!) over any passage of writing, but there are several parts of the opening pages which are we might say, more extreme than others in this.

The opening sentence is deliberately abrupt, brief, sudden, full of a strong beat. Perhaps this was intended as a surprise. It also gives us death in the third word of the whole story. Is this going to be a story about Marley? Or death? We find out later it's not about Marley! Is it about death? In a way, it is about how we might be thought of after we are dead, so we might as well get life right now. But a bit odd that the first word is 'Marley'. Does this signal that Scrooge's downhill path into miserliness starts with Marley?

Whatever it is, it's very arresting to begin a story with a) such a brief, drumming sentence, b) death and c) a self-conscious 'to begin with'.

In paragraph 3, the egotism of Scrooge is given to us partly through the prosody of an extreme and excessive rhythmic repetition of the word 'sole'. It indicates that not only is Scrooge excessive but that he was also on the fiddle. This is confirmed by the ironic commentary on him as being an 'excellent man of business' i.e., a crook.

In paragraph 6, we meet a whole range of musical devices.

It begins with an 'Oh!' (like Beowulf beginning with 'Hwaet!'); a long sequence of '-ing words to describe Scrooge, exaggerated, excessive, extreme writing. (by the way, next sentence would be marked as incorrect by examiners as it has a capital letter, a full stop but NO FINITE VERB! The next sentence switches from 'ing verbs' to '-ed verbs in repetition. In some of the sentences he breaks another rule of so-called 'good writing' he repeats 'and' – partly, I think, to create a speech rhythm.

In paragraph 7, the writing uses Anglo-Saxon style alliteration, moving from one set of alliterative words to another set: e.g., going from 'w' words to 'b' words and then to 'p' words. This gives the writing strong pulse, marking the rhythm by linking the beats to each other. Perhaps this kind of writing has no purpose other than to feel good and to sound good. Perhaps it is to carry us along with the sequence of phrases, in a lyrical way. I don't know!

There is another way in which prosody works, which is by a kind of anti-prosody! Dickens, we know, was very fond of deliberately long, 'otiose' sentences. Some have argued that this is almost ironic, in that he appeared to be over-honouring a subject with seeming pomposity in order to diminish it. It's one of the functions of 'hyperbole' (rhetoric). The sentence in paragraph 4, that begins: 'If we were not perfectly convinced . . .' is 65/66 words long! The first sentence in the story is 6 words long. Clearly Dickens could play with his readers' expectations in this respect: one moment being brief and to the point, the next being digressive and discursive. This enables him to switch tone and switch register (see 10). Like the more conventional prosodic features of repetition of '-ing' words, with their ability to be musical, these are perhaps part of Dickens's attempt to catch the ear, make us 'pay attention'. We talk of 'dull' writing, or 'interesting writing' and perhaps the ability to be musical and to vary sentence length is part of that. I think so.

6. How are people, places, animals etc., 'evoked'?

This is a way of looking at such devices as 'incremental detail', 'digression', speed of being 'in' or 'outside' of a person or thing, whether the method of evoking uses many, few or no adjectives and adverbs. We usually describe a lot of adjectives and adverbs as e.g., 'florid' or 'wordy' and sentences that use few or none as 'spare', 'lean', or 'sparse'.

In paragraphs 6 and 10, we can see Dickens using the incremental detail approach, piling descriptions one on top of the other, linked (as we've shown) by the prosody. Is this 'excessive' in the sense that it offers us some kind of superfluity? One of the techniques of 'gothic' writing is 'excess', excess of emotion, excess of horror, excess of sensation. This writing is perhaps 'gothic' in that it asks of us to follow an excess of sensation (i.e., appeals to the sense). Is this appropriate? Presumably Dickens wanted to say from the outset that Scrooge is an extreme form of something: at this stage that he is 'cold' – an almost Elizabethan way of describing him, according to his 'humours'. We can see in the writing that there are two forces going on – one 'realist' but also non-realist in the self-conscious narration. Perhaps Dickens is flagging up that this is going to have realist elements but that the core story is a fairy story, or fantasy and like these kinds of stories with their giants and goblins, Scrooge is a kind of mean giant (not because he's big, but because he's gigantically mean, and that needs an excessive prose to capture that.)

Something that all novelists have to do is show attributes through action. In paragraph 11, Dickens shows that Scrooge is mean over the incident(s) of the coal shovel. If Bob brings in too much coal, Scrooge warns him that he will fire him. And in the next sentence we see that Bob therefore has to warm himself with a candle. In films and plays, this is sometimes played for laughs. In the cold (!) light of day, however it's terrible, isn't it? Bob is not cold because there isn't enough coal. It's because his rich employer is not prepared to let him burn enough coal. It's a direct act of extreme cruelty. To be fair on those wanting comedy, the final part of the evocation of this relationship between employer and employed, there is a line of irony (grim? or jokey?) Bob uses the candle in an 'effort' to warm himself, but 'not being a man a strong imagination, he failed.'

The omniscient narrator tells that Bob doesn't have a strong imagination, so he can't imagine himself to be warmer. At first this is a narrational 'put-down'. But hang on – no one can imagine himself to be warmer. Perhaps the ironic narration here is intended to mock the attitude that poor people should just imagine themselves to be comfortable rather than Bob being of low intelligence and/or imagination. As we find out a few paragraphs later, Scrooge belongs to the 'Malthusian' mind set that there are too many poor people in the world, that workhouses, prisons and death are the best things to be doing with them. The book as a whole is a critique of this view point or ideology. Perhaps it is appearing in this paragraph for the first time, first with Scrooge and the coal shovel, and the threat of getting the sack, and then with this idea of the 'imagination' being enough to live off (i.e., not!).

Irony, then, is part of how Dickens 'evokes' people and situations.

7. Intertextuality through allusion, motif, trope, rhetoric . . .

Clearly allusive intertextuality comes to us e.g., through the allusion to Hamlet and 'Nature'. The effect of this is partly positional – it places *A Christmas Carol* in a continuity with *Hamlet* and 'Nature'. It says, 'this story is touched by such predecessors and ancestors in literature'.

It's fun to go 'motif-spotting' in any text to see, if you like how has a write plundered the world bank of motifs in order to construct a story. One classic literary motif or device on show here is the 'pathetic fallacy'. Scrooge is 'cold'. 'The cold within him froze his old features' and so is the weather. 'It was cold, bleak, biting weather.' What does the pathetic fallacy do for us as readers? I often think its function is to be all-encompassing, inviting us to think that there is no escape from the 'fallacy' in question. Cold inside and out. Both in 'wide shot' and in 'close up', there is coldness. It also suggests perhaps there's no escape for the protagonist in question unless they can change in a big way. After all, for them to be 'warm' they might have to change the cosmos!

A form of rhetoric on display in this section of the book is 'litotes', descriptions of something by what they're not. Para 8 is tells of what 'Nobody' will do. No one will approach Scrooge and 'say, with gladsome looks, 'My dear Scrooge, how are you?'' There then follows some other examples of 'no'. When this ends, the litotes turns into its opposite 'hyperbole', 'Even the blindman's dogs appeared to know him . . .'. All this has a grand, again 'excessive' way of describing. Is this funny? Comical? Is this 'caricature'? Perhaps. Was this what Dickens wanted or was he a victim of his own ability to write like this i.e., he couldn't stop himself being over-excessive? Is his writing guilty of creating moments for the reader where we might say, 'Yeah,

yeah, we got the point, no need to labour it!'? Some people think so. Another word people have used about this kind of writing is that it's 'self-indulgent'. Is it? Or does it do the job of telling us yet again what an extreme form of meanness is on display here?

Other examples of intertextuality we might 'notice' – it's impossible for someone who knows their nursery rhymes to read 'counting-house' without it linking to the 'king was in his counting house'. 'The fog came pouring in at every chink . . .' is intertextual with Dickens's own writing in 'Bleak House' no matter whether that comes before or after this book. Intertextuality doesn't always work on readers in chronological sequence! It's just links across 'space' not time. I suggested that the alliterative prosody was 'anglo-saxon' derived from that kind of rhythmic, non-rhyming, alliterative verse.

In medieval and renaissance art and literature the idea of Carnival and Lent was personified. Carnival represents warmth, jollity, play, music, food, plenty. Lent was mean, damp, cold, thin, hungry. You can see it played out visually in a painting by Bruegel. Can we say that Scrooge has an intertextual predecessor in 'Lent' and the arrival of the nephew – 'ruddy and handsome, his eyes sparkled', 'he was all in a glow' etc., is at the least a representative of 'Carnival'? Is this one of the themes of the book that what we need (or should have) at Christmas is less Lent, more Carnival (or its Roman predecessor Saturnalia?).

'Once upon a time . . .' is an intertextual device that flags up: 'this is a particular kind of story, because you are familiar with the opening of fairy stories, which begin with these words'. This entitles us to think that this might be a kind of fairy story even though it hasn't felt like this so far. So is this a genre-shift? An example of 'hybridity' in texts when we shift from one genre to another which may create surprise, might be a 'red herring', might cause us to focus in a new way, in order to reflect on what's just been? So, we thought this was going to be a realistic story about a mean guy (OK, gothically described) but in the real world of 'now' with a partner who's just died, who the narrator appears to have known (!) and now it's a 'Once upon a time . . .' story. Will there be fairies and giants in this story then? It raises this expectation.

8. Reveal-Conceal

The particular narrative device of 'Reveal-conceal' can be done in many ways, and it's important because it is how texts 'drag' readers through. They are 'hooks' which pull on us, resulting (if they work) in us wanting to know more, wanting to turn the page.

We might argue that the opening sentence does this. It announces a 'fact' and then undercuts it with 'to begin with'. This of course immediately suggests that there's a lot more to come. Is the fact that Marley is dead, enough to feed into 'to begin with' to make us want more? Might this story be about how or why Marley died? Might it be about the consequences of Marley dying or being dead? It's certainly not an explanation in itself, so we might well be wanting to know about reasons and consequences, aided by the reveal-conceal device of 'to begin with'.

'Once upon a time' is a reveal conceal in the way that I've already described, but of course it's an 'opener' . . . it says, 'this is when . . . but now there's more to come that I haven't told you yet . . . listen!'

Another way to do reveal-conceal is to bring up phenomena that are unexplained, mysterious, (what Freud called 'unheimlich' usually translated as 'uncanny' but meaning literally 'un-homely'). Such invocations to the mysterious are revelations ('here they are') but don't tell alls (conceal). In paragraph 10, 'the houses opposite were phantoms.' A sentence later it tells us that 'Nature' is 'brewing on a large scale'. All this is reveal-conceal: mysterious, not-yet-explained and belonging to the world of the unexplained, inchoate 'nature' at work. Will it be 'Nature' that will have a part to play in this story? Might it be the agent which will help the focaliser, the chief protagonist to resolve his problems? Or will it be the word we met in the previous sentence, 'phantoms'? Whatever it is going on, it's 'brewing', that is: cooking up something not yet cooked.

9. Writerliness

This is the fact of a particular kind of writing drawing attention to the fact that we are reading a piece of writing. As we've seen already, there's a good deal of this going on in these paragraphs: words that indicate story-telling itself: 'to begin with', 'I am going to relate', 'Once upon a time'. We can add in the way in which Dickens conjures up Hamlet and Nature, uses excessive prosody, engages in narrator conversations with himself, talks to the reader as 'you', and so on. These are ways of breaking out of realism, or at least putting realism in tension with writerliness. It positions the reader as someone both inside the text and outside – perhaps at the same time, being moved by the events of the text, whilst being part of the process of it being told. The argument that some make over this is that it enables us to keep a part of ourselves asking why, being evaluative, thinking about ideas . . . just as Dickens hopes that we will as he says in the Preface. In Brechtian terms this is 'alienation technique' or in German Verfremdungseffekt', 'estrangement'.

10. Register

The simplest register switch in texts are between paragraphs of continuous prose description of e.g., action, switching to dialogue, let's say, spoken in non-standard English. Clearly, some of this goes on. But there are other register switches here. The 'I' narrator often uses spoken-word type phrases or words, e.g., 'Mind!' or 'Oh!' and addressing the reader as 'you'. The digressive nature of the 'I' narration is reminiscent at the very least of speech, and the faux 'brings me back to the point I started from' is a classic speech mannerism. The *Hamlet* digression would be 'highfalutin' 'elevated' stuff, if it wasn't for the way Dickens undercuts it with the observation about 'any other middle-aged gentleman'. The rhetorical and prosodic excess are also issues of register because they are in their own ways, ways of invoking other 'voices', the voices of, say, Greek drama, or romantic poetry. There is a constant dance (!) of figurative language, particularly in the descriptions of Scrooge, metaphor, simile and personification – as with the 'cold' in para 6 that has a life of its own, the weather 'biting', and of course the great opener and mock 'writerly' debate about being 'as dead as a door-nail'. All this takes us into the world of literariness itself, which is a 'voice' too.

As I've mentioned, Dickens is very adept at switching from 'excessive' writing (a 'gothic' voice, I've suggested) to more action-led, sparer descriptions as with paragraph 11, when we are in Scrooge's workplace: 'The door of Scrooge's counting-house was open that he might keep his eye on his clerk . . .'. It's very direct, unadorned writing, undecorated writing. These switches, we might say, ask us to follow things in different ways. Heavily adjectival, adverbial, figurative language asks us to follow things often in a very 'sense-laden' way. Spare, action-led sections ask us to follow doing. We watch action being revealed. Dickens makes one paragraph do one thing and the next another. It's a stylistic technique.

11. Dialogue – pragmatics

There is only one bit of true dialogue in this passage, but it's quite significant in one respect. It's interrupted by narration.

A 'cheerful voice' (synecdoche!) says, 'A merry Christmas uncle! God save you!' In our reading (as opposed to the dialogue) this is interrupted by: 'It was the voice of Scrooge's nephew, who came up on him so quick that this was the first intimation he had of his approach.'

Then we hear 'Bah!' said Scrooge, 'Humbug!'

Why the interruption? I would suggest that it's for the same reason that comedians delay gags, whether in the sentence, or at the end of passages. It's to highlight punchlines, or significant lines, to give them welly or weight.

Pragmatically speaking, Scrooge hasn't 'replied to what the nephew has said, he's commented on it. He's not returning a greeting or really retorting. He's saying in effect, 'you saying "merry Christmas' is 'humbug'. The exclamation that comes before it is more direct as 'Bah!' is a push-back along the lines of 'rubbish' or even 'shuttup'.

12. Ideology

En route I've said quite a bit about this. I think there are several key aspects of ideology to highlight though:

1. The role of the 'I' narrator is to say, I think, 'I Dickens, have something important to tell you, I control this narrative, and as I said in the Preface it involves an 'Idea'. It's my Idea. Please listen.'

2. The figure of Scrooge is mythic. He is in the pathetic fallacy, he is described excessively, 'Nature' is invoked in this, and several ancient rhetorical devices take us to a literary landscape. Along with 'Once upon a time . . .' and 'phantoms' we are entitled to expect a fairy story or myth or fable or fantasy?

3. Once into the action, we are significantly in a workplace where the conditions of the employee are crucial. He is a victim of the employer, to the extent that he is not entitled to be warm in the midst of this all-encompassing 'cold'. We might expect this to be at least part of the focus of the drama to come. Will this man, the clerk, survive? Will he ever get what he needs, or will he die?

4. Earlier there were indications that Scrooge is a crook (over how he behaves in relation to Marley's legacy). Does this mean that Scrooge's crookery will be uncovered? Come back to bite him? Or what?

Part 6

Do we need 'grammar' to tell us what *Where the Wild Things Are* is about?

Literary criticism is like an old footballer facing opponents who are schooled in the latest techniques of fitness and tactics. In my lifetime, it has faced the challenge of many new ways of describing and analysing literature and yet, at heart, it is what it's always been, human beings reading, listening, wondering, reflecting.

Anyone who's familiar with my work will know that I'm a fan of such disciplines as narratology, stylistics, pragmatics and intertextuality. I believe that if these schools of theory are broken down into 'trigger questions' that books can be explored in enjoyable ways, which both show how texts are put together but also reveal how the person reading is engaging with that text. Anyone who's been round the houses on this matter over the last 50 years will remember that one challenge the old footballer faced was 'semiology'. Various critics 'discovered' this theory of the sign and believed that some kind of objective route could be found to reveal the final truth about literature. Semiology hasn't disappeared but its challenge to 'lit.crit' seems to have faded. I've argued in one of my blogs, for example, that the categories of 'syntax' and 'paradigm' are useful ways of working 'variation' into writing and that this is what Hollywood does in reworking genres like the rom.com. Even so, semiology hasn't knocked our old footballer out the game.

The latest challenge facing lit.crit. is an old one: it's 'grammar'. Ironically, this challenge hasn't come from young critics wielding theory. It's come from the bastion of power, the government, informed by such people as the Tory journalist, Simon Heffer, whose book, *Strictly English* seems to have delighted Michael Gove. The book resolutely turned its back on anything linguistics had to say about language over the last 50 years, reproduced the 'latinate' model of sentence analysis. This was then translated into a glossary, curriculum guidelines, tests at Key Stage 1 and 2, and, incredibly and absurdly, extended into ways of demanding that children should write. The whole thing was based on the false premise that children's 'grammar' is either 'right or wrong'.

Where does our old 'lit.crit' come into this? Flushed with success over the introduction of 'grammar' into primary schools, there are clear signals coming from government that they want this carried through into the secondary curriculum. Experienced English teachers and advisers, sensing that this is on the agenda are hoping to outflank this by producing documents and books which adopt more enlightened and nuanced ways of 'using grammar' to critique texts, than the Simon Heffer-Michael Gove model. I fear that the reason for doing this is not because there has been a long discussion by linguists, English teachers and advisers about what are the best and most suitable ways of discussing literature. It is, instead, as I've described it, an attempt to outflank the government, cut them off at the pass by showing that it's possible to do this stuff in a better way. My suggestion is that if we take a 'holistic' approach to the exploration of literature, then 'grammar' is only one of many approaches and that the approaches I've described will offer up richer responses than the ones offered by 'grammar'. I would also add that if you read the literary criticism offered by, let's say, the broadsheet newspapers, the *Times Literary Supplement* and the *London Review of Books,* their fascinating and highly readable articles hardly ever refer to 'grammar' as a means of exploring books. It is more often than not as I've described it, the old footballer using the wiles of experience to engage readers.

One text that has come up for grammatical analysis by the new footballers on the scene is *Where the Wild Things Are* (*Wild Things*). This is a book that is of huge interest to me. I've made radio programmes about it, done what I've called a 'marxist criticism' of it on my blog and used it as an example of a three year old's 'interpretation' many, many times on the blog and elsewhere by way of critiquing the crude 'retrieval and inference' model foisted on primary school teachers for the last ten years or so.

On this occasion I want to look at one sentence (the one that my then 3-year old son drew my attention to) and give it some close scrutiny, without using 'grammar'.

(By they way, the reason I keep putting 'grammar' in inverted commas is that the grammar applied by the government is one very narrow, limited, inflexible form, which, I argue, is one of the reasons for it offering so little in helping us explore literary texts. It claims to be a grammar based on structure and function, but my argument is that the 'function' here is merely a function deduced from the supposed logic of sentence and paragraph construction, mostly in 'ideal' circumstances rather than actual usage. Again, I would argue that 'function' needs to be widened to social purpose for 'grammar' to be useful. Otherwise, it keeps returning to being not more than a list of instructions on what should be said and written according to the 'rules' of one usage only: written, formal, continuous prose. I'm writing according to these instructions now, but I'm under no illusion that its reach is highly limited, partly as a consequence that it is this form of language!)

Back to *Wild Things*. Our three year old drew my attention to what I call the 'elbow' of the story. This is the moment when the accumulated challenges and dilemmas of the story reach their peak, the main protagonist now has the biggest decisions to make. (These moments are 'intertextual' in that the history of story determines that we, as readers, demand that 'story' mostly delivers up this 'crunch' moment.

Hollywood has formulas for them and demand that scriptwriters deliver them at a certain exact time in movies. (If ever you want to shred the mystique of literary criticism then look at film script manuals on how to manipulate writing and audience responses!)

The 3 year old's pointer to the crux of the story is the moment after the 'rumpus'. You'll remember that Max has tamed the *Wild Things* and they spend several text-free pages dancing. Those who hope that grammar will reveal all about *Wild Things* will have some difficulty with the text-free pages. However, according to people like William Moebius, Margaret Meek and others who have suggested that the picture book is a remarkable piece of 'multimodal' literature then the 'relay' between text and picture doesn't stop when there is no text. Indeed, it's part of the 'syntax' of the book as a whole, and a key moment in the way in which the book is often read by parents, carers, teachers and children. The rumpus is often 'rumpussed'! The fear of the *Wild Things* is dissipated in the rave. Aristotle, who invented a syntax of drama and tragedy, would have things to say about this.

So, the rumpus comes to an end and the text has the famous line:

'And Max, the king of all wild things, was lonely and wanted to be where someone loved him best of all.'

Our 3 year old, had 'used' this book many times for deep study and reflection, hardly making any comments, said one day, in response to this line, 'Mummy!' I've written about this as an example of 'interpretation' not 'retrieval' or 'inference' because it is neither a correct or incorrect response. The text is very open (I'll come back to this) in how we might respond to its suggestions. There is no 'Mummy' in the text. There is a 'mother' whose sole action at the beginning of the book is to send Max to his room and whose 'experience' is to receive Max's threat to 'eat her up'. There is no internal explanation of reason to think that 'Mummy!' is the 'someone' who would love Max (or the reader) 'best of all'. Repeat: 'there is no internal reason'. In other words, the main way you can arrive at 'Mummy!' as a response is through bringing your own experience to bear. It's not 'textual' or 'grammatical' analysis that reveals this truth to you. By the way, at the end of the story when Max is seemingly rewarded with a plate of hot food, again the text doesn't say who has provided this. It is an 'open' text. It invites the reader to interpret the 'gaps'. It repeatedly uses the device of 'reveal-conceal' in order to invite these interpretations. This is not 'grammatical'. It is a literary device that can be expressed using any number of grammatical methods and yet it is the key way in which we are 'dragged' though a story, wanting to know what happens next.

Back to the line. What is going on in this sentence? Can we ask important questions without necessarily going to 'grammar'?

'And Max, the king of all wild things, was lonely and wanted to be where someone loved him best of all.'

One of the instruments of 'intertextuality' is 'rhetoric' – literary devices which grew up originally as techniques for orators to use in ancient Greece because, it was thought, they had 'effects'. Let's apply rhetoric (not grammar) to the sentence. Max is elevated in the sentence as 'the king of all wild things'. It's a reminder of his status as achieved by his cunning plan to stare at the Wild Things straight in the eyes. It tamed them. Phew! Now the text is reminding us of this achievement. Immediately following this elevation, though, Max is lowered: he is 'lonely'. This is a form of 'bathos', from high to low, (ideally as swiftly as possible). Lovers of 'Macbeth' will remember that the famous gatekeeper scene is often cited as 'bathos' across from scene to scene. This is what's going on here too, from 'King of all wild things' to being a 'lonely' little boy.

Now, without invoking any particular theory, let's look at the rest of the sentence: 'where someone loved him best of all'. Let's ask ourselves a human question: why does it say 'someone'? Why doesn't it say, and he 'wanted to go home', or 'he wanted to go back to his mother', or any other formula you could come up with which would be 'specific'? I have no final answer for this other than that our 3 year old's response tells us something. I suspect that Sendak wanted readers to ask themselves 'who is that someone?' He wanted the text to be 'open to interpretation'. He wanted active reading. This kind of active reading also invites readers to think about their own lives. As I've said, the response 'Mummy' is not from the text alone. It comes from our three year old's life. It is him saying, 'If I was Max, I would miss my Mummy'. The text doesn't say that though. He does the intellectual work to get to that.

Another advantage of saying 'someone' is that invites readers to not just think of a specific 'someone' but also of the general feeling of wanting to be loved 'best of all'. It opens the text out to the general. I notice that online, where this line sits amongst 'great lines' from books, someone has added, 'don't we all!' By saying 'someone', Sendak opens up the possibility that this book is not just about Max but has general significance about such things as 'anger', what we now call 'anger management' (!) and resolution. The suggestion here is that there is a loneliness that needs, (demands?) love from 'someone' to help us arrive at a resolution. The book, then, might also apply to us as adults? Possibly.

What I've done here, then, is not look at the sentence grammatically. I've applied 'rhetoric' (one kind of 'intertextuality'), 'reader-response' by listening to our 3-year old, text-syntax (in my talk about an 'elbow' – again triggered by our 3-year old) and a general speculation about the word 'someone' and what it might reveal. I should add here that again, the 'someone' is part of that literary technique (also 'intertextual') of 'reveal-conceal'. Even as it declared a new idea in the plot (Max wanting to be loved), it 'concealed' who this might be. We might find ourselves wondering, will he find someone who will love him best of all? We turn the page to find out.

I've also drawn attention (through 'narratology') to the way in which texts show how people think. They do this in very different ways. On this occasion the narrator tells us through the word 'want'. ' . . . wanted to be where someone loved him best of all.'

But there's something odd here, isn't there? If this part of the sentence is telling us 'what Max was thinking' then it's highly unlikely he just wanted to be where a 'someone' loved him best of all, isn't it? Wouldn't he have wanted to be with a particular person? Or perhaps not? Perhaps all he did want was a general, inchoate sense of wanting to be loved. Is the text saying, 'anyone would do'? All he wanted was a great big chunk of personalised love? Or is this the narrator/author saying that what we (humans, not just Max) need and want, is for anyone, saying to us, 'you're the 'one' I love'? This is a highly particular and ideological view of how we as humans operate. That is that our means of emotional and psychic survival depends on the specific love of one person. Ironically, the vehicle for this world view is the general word 'someone'! As I say, 'anyone will do'.

Sendak was informed by Freudian analysis. The book is a playing out of the story of how the 'ego' can conquer the 'id', but in so doing sets up a crisis. (The elbow of the book in this line.) The Freudian model of need is very personalised focussing on the prime relationships of boys with mothers and girls with fathers. It suggests that the rest of life is determined by this 'prime' relationship and how it played out in our lives when we are under five.

This one sentence reveals how Sendak used Freudian theory and it gave him 'someone' rather than 'go home' or 'go back to his Mother' so that he can open up our response to this highly ideological view that we all need one person to love us 'best of all'. (I'm not saying here whether this is right, wrong, or any other value judgement). The text at the very least asks us to think about whether that is what I, you, he, she, we (any of these) really do want or need.

Part 7

Some short thoughts on why picture books are so important

The young child hearing the words of a picture book being read, and looking at the pictures all the while, 'knows more' than the voice only saying the words! The child 'sees' what the text is not saying. This is great for a child's self-awareness and confidence.

Parents who share hundreds of picture books with their under-5s enable their children to make cognitive leaps through trying to interpret the logic and meanings suggested by the unstated differences between the pictures and the text.

I think it's much more than 'inference'. It's interpretation, cognition, logic, symbolism, holding several ideas in the head at the same time, the germs of abstract thought through analogy etc.

Curriculum which narrows responses to books to 'retrieval', 'inference', 'chronology' and 'presentation' cut off the 'interpreting response' which explores logic, cognition, emotion, empathy and ideas. Irony: this disadvantages those who didn't have hundreds of picture books!

Tweeter: " . . . early reading books must include words which may be hard to decode to keep a child's interest."

(My reply) . . . or ideas, mysteries, excitements, tensions, fears, loss, hope, yearnings, wishes, dreams, reveries, boasts, downfalls, musicality . . .

Let's not get trapped by the word 'vocabulary'. Language is much more than vocab. What helps children is providing processes (books, games, experiments, outings) that are conceptually rich and which encourage leaps of interpretation.

Every time a child tells a story in response to a story they've read or heard, they're selecting a common element from both and creating or affirming a schema. It's the first step in abstract thought. We should aid this and not cut it off with a plethora of 'retrieval' questions.

Prediction is one of the pleasures of reading. Authors embed deliberate prediction-potential situations in their writing as if to say, 'I hope you do some predicting now!'

Literature can't be dismissed or patronised as 'pure imagination'. It's the mix of feelings and ideas attached to beings we recognise and care about. So literature can enable us to grapple with abstractions while we think we're dealing with emotion. Or vice versa.

Starting from speech bubbles on murals at Pompeii, picture books, cartoons and graphic novels have evolved to tell multimodal stories in ways that ask readers to make leaps of understanding as they hop between text and image.

Picture books enable children to make cognitive leaps between text and picture as they figure out the relationship between word and image. This advances logic, perception, reason . . . and much more.

Part 8

Writing: how? 19 thoughts

1. Year 8, Harrow Weald County Grammar School, 1959: we read Browning's 'dramatic monologues 'and talked about what was told and how. Homework: 'write a dramatic monologue, long, short, prose or poem.' And we could!!! Literature that works is infectious.

2. How do writers of non-fiction research, select material? How do we lay that out in sequences? How do we make sure there are as few ambiguities as possible. How do we distinguish between fact and opinion? How do we invite (or not) readers to debate what we write?

3. Why would it be in anyway sensible to take advice on writing from Gove, Gibb and their pals rather than from e.g., Frank Cotterell Boyce, Philip Pullman, J.K, Rowling, Shirley Hughes, Malorie Blackman, Jacqueline Wilson, David Almond, Jamila Gavin, Michael Morpurgo, Anne Fine, etc.?

4. Many stories have an elbow or crux, the moment when an accumulation of problems has led to a defining moment which in theory could lead to success or failure, good or bad outcomes. These elbows should be almost painful!

5. The questions, who am I? Where am I? When am I? are often good places to start writing, even if it's non-fiction: the 'who' can be e.g., the impersonal narrator of a scientific description. It's still a 'who'!

These questions help define the genre(s).

6. The formulas for 'expected level' of 'good writing' created by the govt are nonsense and could only have been created by people who don't write or are lying about how they write.

7. With jeopardy in writing, always ask who or what is causing it? Who or what is it happening to? How does the jeopardised get out of it? (Or not!) With whose help? (Or not!) And why did we choose that cast to display that jeopardy?

8. Writing relies heavily on the writer assuming readers are constantly predicting. Writers create *possible/probable* outcomes and then confirm, disrupt, ruin these . . . usually done in an unspoken way. Hidden story syntax.

9. Fiction is writing about ideas and feelings attached to beings who readers care about. The feelings emerge out of our varying attachments to what characters do and say with/to each other. Ideas emerge out of a sense of right/wrong, Fair/unfair, in scenes and outcomes.

10. Part of learning to write (which all writers do till the day they die) is 'finding a voice' (or voices). We find these through reading and listening, saying to ourselves: 'I could write like that.' As we imitate, we adapt to suit the purpose. Continuity and change.

11. The 'cliffhanger' is the most extreme form of 'reveal/conceal'. In truth, all writing, even reports, argument, non-fiction , Poetry relies on many, many mini-cliffhangers: moments which 'say' I'm not telling you all, there's more to come.

12. Fiction relies heavily on dramatic irony: situations, states of mind etc., that the writer creates in which a protagonist appears to know less than the reader.

13. All writing is a 'con' in one respect: it pretends to 'reveal' but at the very moment it reveals it 'conceals'. That is: it implies but doesn't say *yet* what's coming next. This is what 'pulls' the reader through a text, thinking 'I want to know more'.

14. In writing, there is no such thing as a good or bad word in itself. It always depends on context and purpose. Will it help me say what I want to say? Will it help me say it in the way I want to? Does it 'do' humour? Sadness? Nostalgia? Anger? Or what?

15. When writing, we ask ourselves if we want to draw attention to the writing itself e.g., through 'self-conscious narrator', deliberate over-description, heavy repetition of sound or word or the metaphorical. Or aim for invisibility through 'sparse' technique.

16. Every part of a sentence or whole sentence has a rhythm. To find it, repeat it out loud several times. When writing, we can ask ourselves if the rhythm 'feels right'. Sometimes, we might want to accumulate detail = running rhythm. Contemplative might = long phrases etc.

17. The moment we start to write we borrow from previous writings: the genre (or mix of genres), the narrative voice, the register (formal, informal, regional, etc.), motifs (e.g., the 'disruptive force', pathetic fallacy), rhetoric (e.g., hyperbole, rule of 3, story syntax (e.g., rising jeopardy).

18. If you write dialogue in fiction you make rhythms between e.g., speakers taking turns, what characters are thinking, descriptions of how they speak, narrations of events, past, present or future. Some texts (or parts of) do all these. Some rely on dialogue standing on its own.

19. Any writer who has chosen a 'narrative voice' has them to decide 'what does this narrator *know*?' If 'omniscient', inside everyone's head? Specific character(s)? Only what can be seen/heard? Or other narrations? 1st person? Multiple? Crucial decisions for all writing.

Part 9

Poetry does . . . some thoughts

We are often asked 'what is poetry?' What happens if we ask instead, 'what does poetry do?'

I ask because we have reached a point in the history of literature where poetry isn't defined by a universally agreed set of rules. Poetry is what, say, a writer, a publisher and a reader think is poetry. Or perhaps it's someone standing up in a public place and speaking certain kinds of things and everyone in the room is agreed that what's going on is poetry.

It is of course possible to pull together a few elements that most (never all) poems seem to conform to but such definitions will either fall apart because of exceptions, or the opposite: other kinds of writing or speaking will be found to use those elements too. So if we say, for example, that poems are pithy and musical. Well, some are, some aren't. And anyway, so are proverbs. If we say poems say things using the best words in the best order, we can say, so does a really good play, a really good novel, a proverb and a brilliant speech. And so on.

So, I suggest that we can move on from that by looking at what poetry does.

Of course, it 'does' different things in different places. A lot (but not all) of my work is in schools so the list below is about what poetry does (or 'can do' or 'could do') in a school setting. It's really about a set of possibilities rather than a set of closed functions.

If you're a teacher and you need to justify why you're doing poetry then perhaps this list will help you do that. On the other hand you might wonder yourself what the point of it is, particularly if you were told at some point in your life that you didn't understand a poem or were made to think you weren't good enough to enjoy poetry.

What follows is about enjoying poetry and living with it and in it – in school or out.

1. Participatory – solo.

Poetry offers groups, classes and whole schools the possibility of doing stuff in a participatory way. Just as we enjoy sport and music in a collaborative way, so can we enjoy poetry using rhythms, choruses, echo-effects, duets, trios, call and response etc., and where this feels non-coercive it can help us feel joined to other people in a good way.

It also offers something almost opposite: we can go solo with poetry. We can, at other times, hunker down in a corner and express something that feels personal, feels as if it just belongs to me, comes from something that 'only I' have experienced. Then, it's up to us whether we share it or not. The benefits of sharing it are that we discover something about ourselves in the reactions of others – maybe it's very strange, (they seem to be saying) or they may be saying that they experienced or thought something similar. The benefits of not sharing it are that it feels as if it's something to do with feeling a bit good or a bit strong about doing something on our own.

2. Puts chunks of language in children's ears.

I don't subscribe to 'cultural deficit theory' or 'linguistic deficit theory' which says that there are millions of children who have 'no culture' or 'no language' and variations on that theme. However, when poetry works with children, they will adopt poems and they become part of their linguistic and cultural 'repertoire'. Of course, in certain circumstances, this could be no better than a load of old totalitarian crap about how great your nation is and how rubbish everyone else is. In other circumstances, where a range of poems from different viewpoints, different cultures are being read and heard, then that's not the issue.

A good deal of poetry is a kind of 'portable philosophy'. That's to say it expresses quite difficult or challenging ideas in ways that can be carried around in your head. Usually, that's because of the musicality of the poem.

3. Suggests as well as tells . . .

Much of education is about 'telling'. It's about certainties, facts, knowledge etc. However, part of who we are as humans is that we exist with each other through suggestion. We imply, infer, allude to things. We use tone of voice, volume, expression and gesture to indicate what we think. A lot (not all) of poetry occupies this space too. A good deal of it suggests that things are being thought, said or felt without tying it down completely. In an ideal world, we would think and talk about these things without having to tie them down to tests with specific answers to what this or that word of phrase suggested.

4. Doesn't have to tie up a story – leave it hanging.

Narrative poems don't have to have endings. Most teaching of story-writing is aimed at children includes ways of winding up, closing and concluding stories. Sometimes this results in forced endings that don't work. I believe that nothing ends in real life. The whole point about life is that it's lived socially which means that when anything ends, something carries on – as carried by other people. So, satisfying as stories are, they don't express that notion. Poems can. They can hang in the air, leaving us as readers to 'carry on', imagine what is implied, or what might have happened next. Or indeed, we are part of the 'carrying on'.

5. It can be about a state of mind, how you feel.

Many poems for the last century are not really narrative in the usual sense of the word. They express a state of being. Famously, Adrian Henri wrote 'Love is . . . ' which was a list rather than a narrative. Yes, you could claim each of the 'Love is . . . ' lines is itself a kernel of a narrative but overall, it's about a notion, 'love'. But poems can also be about how you (singly or collectively) might be feeling at a particular moment in a particular place, a fragment of consciousness – a notion in itself first elaborated by Henry James's brother!

6. Can make a statement of belief.

Many poems can be statements of what 'I' or what 'we' believe. They can be declamations, or declarations. Think 'Howl' by Ginsberg. So the kind of space that the phrase 'let's write a poem' gives you is also one that can be 'let's write down what we believe about . . . '. One of the great 'poems' of the 20th century, I believe, is Martin Luther King's 'I have a dream' speech or Pastor Niemoeller's statement 'First they came for . . . '.

7. It borrows language from everywhere else, so good for a sense of parody, fun, use of language for many purposes not just one.

I think many or most poems have been produced by crows. Crows are scavengers and improvisers. They go about hunting for stuff that may well be edible. Poets are like that with language-in-use. It's not just that poets collect words. I think that's misleading. I think poets keep spotting words-in-use in the signs, notices, cliches, conversations, observations that people make . . . or also in particular professions' use of language, or 'types' like e.g., grandmothers. And poets also scavenge all previous poems for shapes and forms of poems to use, sonnets, call and response, question and answer, montage, haiku etc. These are shapes and sounds that can be scavenged and used.

This can make the process of making poetry in schools a way of using, collecting and critiquing the language-use that children and students find around them. This makes it different from most other kinds of language-use in schools which is mostly about learning how to use language in prescribed and received ways e.g., this is how you write up an experiment, this is how you write an essay, this is how you write a 'recount'. Poetry-writing can be the opposite: look at how that language-use is saying its stuff . . . how can we use that, parody it, alter it, change it, criticize it?

8. Great for giving concentrated activity in story, recount, events . . .

Life, stories, films, plays, games pass by very quickly. Poems can freeze moments. If we think it's valuable or useful to reflect on life, storeis, films, plays, games etc., then poems can help you do that. They can freeze-frame a moment and ask or tell us things about that moment: what am I thinking? why am I thinking that? what else could I be thinking that would help me get out of that moment? And so on. The most famous 'moment' in action is Shakespeare's 'To be or not to be . . . ' and we can all write poems (musicals do it with songs) which freeze the moment like that. Perhaps it's a way of concentrating thought in the midst of action.

9. Can open up possibilities of other worlds – leading to nonsense.

Nonsense is new sense, experiment with things, environments, state of mind.

Probably all the arts open up possibilites. Nonsense worlds are like alternative worlds, alternative uses of language. This offers up the possibility of experiment, and of not treating the known world as fixed and unchangeable. Nonsense suggests to me that we can shift things around. It's probably an illusion but it's a provocative and interesting place to live in in short bursts. Unpredictability feels good in the midst of highly predictable circumstances like, let's say, in the midst of timetables or itineraries.

10. Can be personal while you're thinking you're talking about someone or something else. (It 'deflects' while it 'reflects'.)

A psychological process thought by some as being valuable is to allow ourselves to reflect on things about ourselves even as we think we're not. So, if I reflect on the abandonment of Hansel and Gretel, I might well think I'm exploring those feelings in 'them' and not in 'me'. But really what's happened is that I've been 'deflected' in order that I might 'reflect' freely with less inhibition than if I was asked to reflect on my own feelings i.e., 'deflect to reflect'. Poetry reading and writing can help people do this.

That said, it can also offer the opposite, the space to 'confess'. We can use poetry to say the unsayable, the things I can't or won't say or wished I had said, or would say if I could etc.

11. It can be a carrier of culture, the thing that identifies you.

Great for cross-cultural sharing, discovering about others.

All poetry is an expression of who we are culturally. It does this by means of the language it's expressed in and the forms of the poems. They all belong within specific cultures and mixtures of cultures. These can be traced, they have histories. The 'sonnet' has a history and if I write one in a certain way, I'm saying something about the cultures I have inherited and the ones I'm part of.

Because the elite culture of, say, Britain, is invisible to those who participate in it, it's become customary to treat e.g., Caribbean poetry as if it alone carries culture, while poems of the elite in Britain are just poems or 'literature'. This is really just a con.

Poetry offers us the possibility of sharing cultures in quite explicit and co-operative ways. Poems often draw attention to this through specific uses of language or mention of beloved objects, descriptions of places, memories of historical events.

12. With 'figurative language' (metaphors, similes, personification etc.) it can invite children to think what things in the world around them are 'like' each other, even when you think they're not.

Metaphors and the rest are really a form of philosophy. They are each invitations to find similarities and differences in things. Part of the struggle of being human is to find and understand what is similar what is different in the things and people around us. Human beings are constantly trying to spot, understand and learn from patterns. Making metaphors (similes and the rest) is one way we do that. I read the opening of 'Dulce et Decorum est' ('Bent double like old beggars . . . ') as a plea by Wilfred Owen to get us to see the degradation being experienced by the men in the trenches. He seems to be saying to me, 'Look, the young men you saw leave Britain have been turned into old men, and instead of being feisty guys with guns, they are now begging, stooped, pleading . . . ' You can say that in a speech but metaphorical language can be a plea that you see things in a particular kind of way, because this or that is 'similar' or 'different' from what you thought it was.

13. Makes familiar things unfamiliar, unfamiliar things familiar (shakes up the world as you know it, challenges, surprises.)

These are sometimes taken as the essence of poetry. Poets make the things we know unfamiliar (often but not always through metaphor, simile, personification etc.) Poets also find unfamiliar things and tell us about them in ways that we come to know them, feel them or understand them.

You could argue that if education just did this, it would have done a good job.

14. Offers great talking points . . . (but must have open-ended questions or no questions!)

A mini-circle time.

I can't speak for all poets, but I know that the main reason why I write poems is that I would hope that for many readers any poem I write offers readers something to think and talk about. They are a way of opening a conversation. If a teacher is looking for ways of helping children talk about things then poems are as good a way as any of starting conversations. However, this will only happen if teachers don't ask questions they already know answers to.

15. Great for 'sampling' or 'anthologising' or 'displaying' and diy dealing with texts.

Making it your own, investigating, collecting, browsing.

Poems are great for doing all of the above – chopping up, collecting, sampling, quoting, performing in sequences, in contrast with each other and so on. This can be a very free sort of activity. Again, if education is to do important things, I can think of nothing more important than passing on the talent of good browsing. Browsing, after all, is the business of scanning and surfing, choosing and ordering 'text', passages, pages, chapters, books, so that you can use them for your own purposes. Poems offer very pleasurable ways of doing this.

16. Mysterious e.g., in its musicality, evocation of other worlds.

Not everything in the world is obvious.

Most of education is concerned with certainties. However, behind a lot of the certainties are uncertainties. So we can describe scientifically how and why leaves fall off deciduous trees and how and why evergreen trees do that differently but it's much harder to explain why there are deciduous and evergreen trees. We can of course just say, 'well there just are' and that's part of 'variation' in the universe. But there is an element of mystery to it. Because poems don't have to be certain (they can be) then they're good at mystery. Sometimes this is an interesting place to be.

17. Poems often work by placing one picture or image or event next to another without giving cause and effect. In, say, a historical account, we tend to do the opposite. One picture of event is linked by causal words like 'because' or 'the reason why' or 'the consequence' and so on. In poetry, you don't have to do that. You can leave that to readers to speculate about. This grants a lot of power to readers, provided we give readers (children, students) the space to do the speculating without worrying that they've got the right answer.

18. Though we often talk about poetry being dense, difficult, full of conundrums etc. It can also be amazingly accessible, not daunting. It can offer ready access to the written language, to complex ideas in very accessible ways. This is the proverbial, populist side of poetry expressed through e.g., folk poetry, folk song, proverb and those poets how inherit those traditions.

Part 10

Why Writing Matters

The following is taken from a talk I gave, for the Royal Society of Literature, to celebrate the first National Writing Day, 21 June 2017:

We cannot know everything. We cannot remember everything. Each of us cannot know everything there is to know about ourselves. Each of us cannot know everything there is to know about everyone else.

For much of the time, this doesn't matter. We're not bothered by it. When there are things we don't know, we can ask other people. Or we can go to the internet, or a book, or a bit of paper with something written on it. Same goes for things we don't remember: what's the name of that trombone player who played in Jools Holland's Orchestra? I say to my wife. If she knows, fine. If not, use a search engine.

Writing, then, has the function of storing up stuff, partly or perhaps mostly because we can't store it in our heads: we can't know everything. We use writing to compensate for our own deficiencies. I like that. Writing helps us. Writing is our prop.

But what if it's something we want to know about ourselves . . . like:

Why am I sad?

Or: What would I do if I was told that soldiers were coming to take me and my family away?

Or: What if I realised that a moment in a hospital when a doctor said to me, in his American accent: 'Technically, you're dead', was so absurd, yet so truthful and turned the previous 15 years on their head and created a new life for the next 35?

Take any or all of these what-ifs: might I not look for some way of grappling with them so that I could investigate them, understand them, remember them and reflect on them so that I can find out what they were for, what did they mean, and where do they fit in with everything else?

I think I might.

And one way – (and it is only one way, there are many others) – might be to join something that the writer Emile Zola called (I don't think he was the first) 'the republic of letters'? The reading-writing community: the great gang of people across the globe and back through history who read and write; write and read; read, write, and talk, – in any combination of these.

Let's go back to those questions. The first was:

'Why am I sad?'

If you don't know me, the only way you can help me with this question is to ask me questions. If you're not there to do that, I might try reading what others have written about being sad. These might be memoirs, biographies, or poems, or great epics, absurd stories, jokes – writings about people who were sad and what they did about it. In which case I'll be pleased that others thought that they wanted to write about such things. I may well find that what they wrote was enlightening or helpful. That's another way in which writing is useful. I can use what others write.

On the other hand, I might take a piece of paper and write at the top, 'Why am I sad?' And underneath that I could try to answer that question. I could try to do that by describing this sadness: what does it feel like?

Or I could try to think of the things that make me sad and simply write them down.

If I didn't want to feel sad quite so often or quite so much, I might write down some things that make me less sad, or make me happy, or would make me less sad if such things were to happen.

At the end of all this, the thing that was quite unmanageable and at times mysterious, inaccessible and overwhelming might at the very least be less mysterious. Something swirling and formless and undefined – even menacing – might become rather plain and ordered, even enumerated as if it was a shopping list.

And there's nothing wrong with shopping lists. Far from it. I love shopping lists. I'd be lost without shopping lists. Thanks to all in my life who've given me shopping lists.

Back to the sad list.

If I had done as I said and written it on a piece of paper, I could fold it up and put it in my pocket and when I got the train to work, I could take it out, and look at it and ask myself whether that was me on that bit of folded paper? Did I get 'me' right? What did I miss out? What did I exaggerate? What did I minimise? If I did that, I would, in some bizarre way, be comparing myself with myself; this is what I would call 'investigating myself'. If I so chose, I could show someone else. I could say, 'I wrote this about my being sad.'

All sorts of things might happen now: that person – or it might be a group of people – might get to work on it: they might check whether

I was telling the truth: did that really happen? They might say that they were moved.

People often say that.

They were 'moved'. We can take that metaphor at face value: they were in one place – in one mood, if you like – before they read something – then they were moved to another place, to another mood. Something else that writing can do.

Or: they might respond by telling me a story. If I'm feeling particularly egotistical, this might irritate me. If I'm feeling more rational, I might listen carefully to that story and think about how or why it's similar to, or different from mine. It might remind me of a story of my own that I didn't put on the original bit of paper and I might tell that too, making a note to myself that I must write that one down later. We are then riffing on sadness. Finding the bones of sadness, creating maps of sadness. The hollow husk-like word 'sadness' becomes fleshy: full of talking pictures, sounds and smells. I will also discover that the sadness that I called mine, the sadness I may well have hugged to myself (even though I said to myself it was unwanted), bears a family resemblance to other people's sadnesses. Together we will be giving shape to sadness, or, if you prefer, redefining it.

This is the republic of letters: reading, writing; writing-reading; talking, writing . . . My next question was very different: it was a 'what would I?' question. "What would I do if I was told that soldiers were coming to take me and my family away?" I often wonder what percentage of our life we spend absorbed by the kinds of mental activity which draw us into wondering things like: what would I do if I was in a given situation? what would I do if I was that kind of person? in that state of mind, in that place, with those people, with those challenges, with those events . . . ? The main word we have for this is 'reading' – though it can be watching and listening or spectating – or even acting, as in taking on a role, role-playing.

So I asked a question about soldiers coming. I guess anyone listening to me has read books, or seen movies about such things. There may well be people listening for whom such things have happened, they've lived through them. And for others – and this is my situation – it's happened to people in my family, in the past. Usually, we are appalled and horrified by such things. We might wonder whether we have the resources and strength to cope, whether we would know how to both help ourselves and help others. And if this feeling of "wondering what we would do", mattered a good deal to us, if we are really bothered about it, either because we've met people or know people in such situations, it might become urgent enough to feel summoned to write about it.

Let's think about that: an urgency to feel summoned to write about it.

It's hard to express this urgency. It is not simply a matter of the thing itself: the incident or the idea demanding to be written – though I have to say that those of us who write are a bit inclined to express it that way. Less glamorous, is the matter of knowing how to be summoned. Put it this way, when you read a lot, certain kinds of experiences, certain moments, certain angles on life, certain views of people's faces, hillsides, arguments, jokes, proverbs, streets, boats, armchairs, Friday night take-aways . . . appear to you as things we might call 'writeable-about'. They come wrapped within stories and poems that unfold in ways that have been folded that way before. Or, you might find a seemingly new experience threaded through with something you've already read. It's what Roland Barthes called "writing with the 'already written'." Not very glamorous but in its own way quite comforting, even exciting: the world is full of millions of stories waiting to be taken by you or me as the 'already written'. Or, at the very least we can compare the already written ones with the ones we think of as so personal, so unique. No harm in that.

My third question was:

What if I realised that a moment in a hospital when a doctor said to me, in his American accent: 'Technically, you're dead', was so absurd, yet so truthful and turned the previous 15 years on their head and created a new life for the next 35?

This happened to me. I've told it. I tell it quite often, I've written about it. I'm going to write about it again. In one sense, I do this in a fairly unreflective way. I don't keep saying to myself: why am I telling this story? I enjoy the self-evidently absurd quality of a doctor telling me I'm dead even though I am standing in front of him. A doctor of all people. Don't they know the difference between life and death? What was all that training for if they don't know the difference? There's another added absurdity in the story in that before he told me that I was dead, he told me that his name was Gesundheit. It's a German word meaning good health and it's what some Germans say to you when you sneeze: 'Gesundheit!'. Dr Gesundheit was telling me I was dead.

That's the story. Or part of it.

No need to reflect on it. A story like that does some kind of job all on its own. If you're a writer, you hope and pray that a Dr Gesundheit will come along every day and do things like tell you you're dead. The great fear for all of us who write is that nothing will happen. We'll be in a room of nothingness in which nothing does anything. Hour after hour. Day after day. There won't even be any 'already-written' lying about or in our heads to feed off. Just anti-Roland-Barthes, one long nothing-already.

But let's say I do choose to reflect on this story. Why do I tell this story and keep writing about it? I'll try to answer that. The story involves a transformation and we all like a good transformation. We often think of our lives as being mostly so even-steven that a bit of transformation is a wonder. Even going bald is a wonder. My transformation was from someone who walked about cold, swollen, slow, almost inert, to someone jumping about like a firecracker. However, the Jumping Jack was a replica of the person who had existed before the swollen, slow, almost inert one came into existence. That's three stages in a life, three ways of being. I was the Third Man.

Oh Ovid, writer of the *Metamorphoses*, you should have been there to see it.

(There I go again, back with the already-written.)

Now the cause of these transformations in this story were chemical. The uncomfortable truth about our lives, about our very being is that ultimately our bodies are chunks of matter in which, and on the surface of which, trillions of chemical reactions take place. In my case one part of me chose to eat another part, the part that is called the thyroid gland. That something so chemical should have resulted in something so much to do with that mystical thing we call our 'personality' was a rude awakening. How dare I be reduced to chemical equations, me with all my individuality? It was in its own way a wonder, and wonders interest us to write about or read. If you know of a wonder, write about it. If you know of a transformation, write about it. People will want to read about that. Even going bald.

My state of mind as the Third Man was itself problematic. In all the time I was the Second Man how much did I miss out on? That is, if I hadn't started to eat myself, and had stayed being the First Man? Unanswerable. But surely I had lost something, hadn't I? And was the Third Man the same as what the First Man would have been? Surely not. There is no such thing as an experience that hasn't happened. By definition, an experience has happened and somewhere inside the Third Man was the Second Man, no matter how inert that Second Man had become. Knots like these, especially unanswerable ones are good for writing about. We are interested in knots. The psychiatrist R.D. Laing once wrote a book full of them. He called it *Knots*.

Myth is a way of exaggerating things. Or it can also be a way of turning things into their essence. It can, say, take fear or dread and turn it into a scenario in which if you look into a creature's eyes, you'll turn into stone. You probably know that one. The dread we feel, or even create for ourselves, is put onto the powers of a mythical creature who makes you petrified – which actually means turned to stone.

If I do reflect on my Third Man experience, it is in its own way mythic. We all have stages: we are all second, third, fourth, fifth people. We move through phases and transformations in our lives. It's just I had one that was more extreme, more exaggerated, more essential than most. It can then stand for , or represent something other than itself: it can stand for what others feel. Possibly. If I write it, and someone else reads what I wrote. Perhaps it's mythic.

To know this about what you write, or at the very least, hope that it might, is to widen the purpose of writing into something to do with humanity and not just me, me, me. That is: what I write may be about more than what I've written. It represents much more, it stands for much more.

Now, a question: how do we understand what writing does for those that read it?

I co-teach an MA in Children's Literature at Goldsmiths, University of London. In one part of the course we ask our students, most of whom are themselves teachers, to devise a research project. They can come up with any proposal which will involve taking literature to children and young people – (and let's not forget, literature is not some kind of abstract quality that floats around on Mount Olympus – but is stuff that real people, living in the world, have written). The students investigate what appears to interest them, or take them towards new understandings about what writing is for, what it can do.

We encourage them to record the children, to transcribe what the children say and do and then to analyse these transcripts. What do the children say to each other? How are they affected by the kinds of questions they are asked by adults? What kinds of questions do the children themselves come up with? Are there indications in how they respond that tell us about the kinds of thinking they are capable of?

What do they select from the books and why? There are countless books about what is called 'comprehension'. There is a whole raft of tests which supposedly tell us how children 'comprehend', but when you come face to face with the actual things that children say, you cannot fail to realise just how complex the matter of reading and talking about reading is. Yet, this is the very point at which writing is doing its work. This is where writing matters.

The academic and researcher, Carol Fox, says this: 'We need to remember that before children have the conventions of different discourses mediated to them through school subjects, narrative must "do for all". Until the non-narrative genres have been learned, children use story to sort out their own knowledge and ideas.'

I understand that this is an academic language so I'll translate: We need to remember that before children get to know that there are ways in which we chop up the world into 'subjects' like geography, chemistry or philosophy, each with their own way of describing and investigating the world, telling stories has to cover or include all these subjects and ways of thinking. Children use stories to sort out what they know and what they think – and even how they think.

Earlier in this passage, Carol Fox says that the children in her research project, used storying to work out their own 'classificatory systems, their forms of reasoning and argument, their observations of natural and physical laws, their concepts of number, size, shape and so on, even their awareness of moral and metaphysical possibilities'.

That's a lot to carry. Put another way: writing has a lot to do.

I'll start with 2 and 3 year olds who more often than not come to writing accompanied by pictures. I say 'accompanied by' but in truth the words and the pictures twine around each other, affecting each other. These two and three year olds are talking about the first picture in *Where the Wild Things Are*. You may know it. The student is researching the idea of showing a few pictures of a book before reading it to them, in order to see if this will hook the children more into the whole book than by simply reading it to them. So, in this first stage, the children see in the picture that there is a child dressed in some kind of animal suit; he's coming downstairs after a dog; there is a washing line; and hanging from it is a long white strip of some sort; and a teddy bear is hanging from the line.

The children are interested in the white strip hanging from the line. They think it might be a slide. Then one of them reckons it's a towel. He thinks that it's a towel because it's hanging on a line. Causation. Causation is so much part of our adult lives, we forget that 2 year olds have to learn it.

Explaining what's going on in a book, is one way to learn causation. One boy starts to rub his hair and says 'Wet'. The children swap instances of being wet: wet hair, going out and getting wet, wet clothes and wet towels. The book is a spur to rediscovering something going on in the material world. They seem to agree that that's what the line is there for, to put wet things on like towels. But the teddy poses a problem. If he's hanging on the line it must be because he's wet. How did he get wet? Why is he wet? Maybe, one suggests that he's been magicked outside, got wet and is on the line now to get dry. Cause and effect. Then their attention turns to the boy in the story and one says that he's got pointy feet and the pointy feet are going to hurt the dog. One boy leaps to his feet and acts out being the boy, the others copy him. The children are concerned the boy in the picture may hurt the dog. Acting it out is a way of living the story, finding out what it feels like to be the protagonist. Yet another important function of writing: giving us an opportunity to try out other ways of being, exploring possibilities in life.

As my student suggests, the children's level of engagement will be a fertile ground on which to read the story as Maurice Sendak has written it. They have engaged with the material world of the story very closely, but with this pointy feet thing, they have also spotted something edgy, difficult and not too pleasant. The pointy feet might hurt the dog. They are concerned. They start to wonder what it would feel like, if you were the dog. Empathy.

But there's something else going on. There is an atmosphere surrounding the book in this room full of two and three year olds which says that a piece of writing is not something closed-ended and fixed but that it is something you can debate and discuss. There might be alternative interpretations, varying feasible views. Just because it's a published book and it's in the hands of a significant and important person – a teacher – it doesn't mean that you can't explore it in the same way as you might explore a beach. Writing is territory laid out for us, with a label attached, saying, 'Please explore.'

There is a story called *Awkward Aardvark* by Mwalimu illustrated by Adrienne Kennaway, which tells of an Aardvark who keeps the other animals, (the mongoose, the monkeys, the lion, and the rhino), keeps them awake at night by snoring and nothing the animals can do will get him to stop. In the end some termites eat away at the bottom of his tree, Aardvark falls out of the tree, gets very angry and eats the termites, before the ones that survive scurry away into their holes. From that day till now, Aardvark has switched. He sleeps by day and comes out at night to eat termites.

Two girls aged 6 talked about this story using three strategies: Does this story remind you of anything that has ever happened to you? Does this story remind you of anything you've ever read before? Do you have any questions to ask anyone in the story? or the author? Heather Rose asked Shireen did the Aardvark story remind her of anything that had ever happened to her or that she had heard about? Shireen said her dad snored so her mum made a plan to stop him snoring. She took a video of him in the night of him snoring and he stopped snoring.

Heather Rose tells some stories about how she annoyed her parents and spins a tale about being told to leave home.

Traditional criticism of literature would rule all this out as irrelevant. It would say that it's not explaining how the writing works, it doesn't explain how 'effective' it is and therefore is not engaging with the writing. (You'll know that routine: first we tell children a bit of writing is 'effective' then we ask them to say why it's 'effective' even if the children don't think it is 'effective'.)

Now, consider what we do at any time in our life, in hundreds of different circumstances. I tell you a story and you tell me one in reply. This is what has happened here. Shireen has replied to the *Awkward Aardvark* story with one of her own. As part of doing that, she has selected an element from the Aardvark story and matched it to one in her own life. It is in its own way a form of generalisation through analogy. In this case, it's: 'snoring and how to stop it'. This is part of the process by which writing helps to produce wisdom. Not simply as pre-packaged messages, but as motifs and scenarios which we compare to others.

Later in the conversation, the two six year olds reverse roles and Shireen quizzes Heather Rose and Heather Rose says that the Aardvark story reminds her of another story called 'The slimy slowly slow sloth'. Note: this appears to be her invention, or we might say, a new bit of writing. It's partly based on a character in an Eric Carle story. In other words, she uses that character, to make up a new story. Shireen now asks her: What happened in that book that was the same in the other book?

Heather Rose says, 'Well it wasn't an Aardvark, it was a sloth. The sloth kept snoring, and woke all the other animals up at night.'

Shireen says, 'Did it have a big nose like the Aardvark?' and a bit later, 'What did they do to stop the sloth snoring?'

What's going on here is that without a teacher asking these children to retell the plot of *Awkward Aardvark*, without asking them to pick out 'significant' or 'effective' parts, through storying we can hear Shireen selecting and using key motifs of the Aardvark story in order to compose her questions for Heather Rose. In the jargon, she has 'internalised the strategies and structures of the story' and turned them into questions. Sure enough, on cue, Heather Rose then comes on strong: 'All the animals decided to make a plan and it was quite a good one and they tricked the sloth that she was going to have a baby and she had to go to the vet . . . [there 's a bit of a digression at this point . . .] and then the animals made a trap and the ants ate him.'

'That's really sad,' says Shireen.

Again, you can see that Heather Rose has taken a motif from the Aardvark story – ants eating away at things – reversed the original motif – and ends up with a new story.

At the heart of all this there is something going on about morality: various kinds of ideas about tit-for-tat justice.

These are based at least in part on some real-life experiences that she had recounted earlier in the conversation about annoying her parents.

So, as Carol Fox says, reading and telling stories involve a lot more than meets the eye. Knowledge of the material world: – such as termites or ants nibbling away at things; knowledge of human behaviour: – the fact of snoring, and the fact that many of us are irritated by others snoring, the difficulty of knowing how to get people to stop, the use of tricks to get your own way, the tendency for us to do tit for tat ways of

83

settling things and so on. These two six year olds have explored these matters mixing writing, reading and talking as a way of investigating, and ordering the world around them.

When we open the doors to our own experiences, swapping stories as a way of unpacking the ideas and motifs at the heart of, say, a written story, even the youngest children will select and generalise through analogy. It may not always look like it, but analogy is in its own way a form of abstract thought. The people doing it, (in this case very young children) are finding common ground and differences between specific instances. Conclusions can be drawn. Writing is doing its work.

By the way, think back to Heather Rose saying that her story is about a 'slimy slowly slow sloth'. Eric Carle's story is called, "'Slowly, slowly, slowly,' said the sloth." Heather Rose has clipped the 'sloth' and the 'slowly' and attached her own arrangement of words to fit it: 'slimy slowly slow'. This process of clipping and rearranging is a great way to start writing. It's what writers do in their notebooks or on their walls. One of the places where a lot of writing goes on where there is hardly ever this kind of clipping and rearranging is on classroom walls. Instead, you'll see advice about 'wow words' and advice about 'fronted adverbials'. No fault of teachers. This advice comes from what is laughingly known as the 'expected levels' of writing deep in the heart of the government's notion of what is good writing. Interestingly, when people in government decide what good writing is, they don't consult writers.

You may know this poem:

I, too, sing America.

I am the darker brother.
They send me to eat in the kitchen
When company comes,
But I laugh,

And eat well,
And grow strong.

Tomorrow,
I'll be at the table
When company comes.
Nobody'll dare
Say to me,
"Eat in the kitchen,"
Then.

Besides,
They'll see how beautiful I am
And be ashamed—

I, too, am America.

– *I, Too*, Langston Hughes

I invited a group of 13 and 14 year old London school students to read it and talk about it using my three facilitating questions: Does it remind you of anything from your life? Does it remind you of any other stories, poems, plays and the like? Do you have any questions to ask of someone in the story or the writer him or herself? Their first reaction was to recount some irritating events in their own lives when their parents had invited friends over and told them that they had to eat somewhere else. This was annoying and unfair, they said. They spent some time on this irritating fact. It really annoyed them. In other circumstances, any of us might have said, yes, yes, yes but let's get back to the poem. The poem is not about teenagers feeling miffed that they miss out when their parents invite their mates over. But I didn't say that. My attitude was that they, as white school students had found common ground with a poem that speaks of the 'darker brother': they were making analogies, finding their own ways to arrive at a concept to do with exclusion and the unfairness of that.

Then, they moved on to the second question about whether it reminded them of any other texts and to start off with. Not a lot. No, there was nothing they could think of. But then one boy called out – I seem to remember, he stood up – and said, 'I've got it. This is Martin Luther King. And the "I had a dream' speech".'

The others were impressed. They looked back at the poem and discussed why this boy might be right – or not. They agreed that there were similarities in what was being said.

In this case, these older students have seen that writing can tell stories that are at one level about itself, that is: about the events, people, images of the story itself, but at another level, these events, people and images can represent something bigger than itself. It carries ideas in what it tells. I haven't told these school students that. They've discovered it through accessing other writings in their heads. And it's not as if Martin Luther King is the model for the poem. Langston Hughes wrote the poem before Luther King made his 'I had a dream speech'. What does this tell us? It reminds us that writing can escape from the limits of time. In our conversations and thoughts, writing can criss-cross time.

When I work with people to encourage them to write, one thing I say is that when you read something, say to yourself, 'I could write something like that.' That 'something like that' conceals a lot. It can mean: 'something that sounds like that', or 'something with that kind of shape', 'something with that kind of plot', 'something with that kind of person or creature in it', 'something with that kind of scene' ,'something with that kind of outcome', or indeed 'anything that comes to mind while I was reading' or 'anything that comes to mind when I sit and think about what was written there'.

It's one of the most powerful triggers for writing. It's like that bit of apparatus I remember from the physics lab in my school: a spark leaps from one pole to another. Find the spark. Let the spark happen.

If you can't immediately think how to write, I'll say this: talk with your pen. Just write what you would say. Use your spoken voice and turn it into writing. Talk with your pen.

I'll finish by telling you about that I wrote:

Today
The rain has died
My shoes have died
The sun has died
My coat has died
The earth has died
Today.

One day
The rain will flower
My shoes will laugh
The sun will sing
My coat will fly
The earth will dance
One day.

I am very fond of this poem. It started out inspired by two things, a photo of a couple of people looking up at a tree. They are in what is known as a 'ghetto'. The Nazis put the Jews in the countries they occupied, into parts of towns where they couldn't leave. They were like huge open-air prisons. There was hardly any work, hardly any food and bit by bit thousands of people died.

My thought at looking at the photo with some children was that this photo – and some others needed a kind of extreme writing that I called 'impossible writing'. Here impossible things would happen.

The people in the photo are full of joy. And yet, because I knew it was taken in the ghetto, it's a sad photo.

I wanted to express all these things in a short poem. I thought of the weather, the trees, and because of some other well-known photos coming from this time, I thought of coats and shoes. I thought of despair and hope; hope and despair. Which way round shall I put it? In some ways, these stories from this time are full of despair. But we can't live on despair. We have to have hope or there is no point in going on, so I decided to do despair then hope.

Today would be despair, because, I figured, these people would know of people dying around them – or, even worse – being taken off on railway trains never to be seen again. In fact we looked at photos of those too. Tomorrow would be hope. The people in the photo looked happy and hopeful. There was fruit on the trees.

So with all these different elements, I wrote the poem. As you can see, it's made up almost entirely of 'impossible writing'. Also tucked away in the back of my mind are the paintings of someone called Marc Chagall. He painted scenes from his childhood from a time when millions of Jews like him lived in the Russian and Polish countryside in small farms and villages. In his pictures, happy people fly, and the colours suggest a thriving, vibrant life. My own great-grandparents came from the places that Chagall painted, and others ended up in ghettos like the one in the pictures.

In the back of my mind I think I wanted to suggest some of this. These are worlds that I never had, was never part of, being safe and sound in London born after the Second World War was over. It's somehow on the other side, in some kind of dream-nightmare world.

That's why it's 'my' shoes and 'my' coat that have 'died'.

But, I always think, the world doesn't have to be like that, In fact, it must never again be like that, for anyone anywhere. By saying 'the earth will dance', I'm saying just that. It's not just me, or my coat and shoes that will laugh and fly but that the whole world will dance.

When I look back at a poem like this, I know that many people reading it won't get from it, what I've put into it. How could they? They might not have seen the photos I'm talking about, they won't know my personal family history, they might not know Chagall's pictures – or if they do – they might not connect them to the poem or me.

So, do I think the poem is pointless? No. I think instead that if you write mysterious poems, that have impossible writing in them, people make meanings out of them that are similar or related to my meanings. Maybe they will pick up on the contrast between despair and hope. Maybe they will see that there are ordinary things like coats and shoes alongside universal things like the sun and the earth and they will see that this is about people and the world. Maybe all sorts of other pictures will come to their minds of, say, street carnivals, or music festivals, or famine followed by plenty.

That's all OK by me. Poems are always a mid-way point between poets and readers. The poet pours in his or her meanings. The reader picks up the poem and put in his or her meanings and the two sets of meanings intermingle. That's what a 'reading of a poem' is. It's the intermingling of two sets of thoughts: the poet's and the reader's.

Postscript

One of the key ways to stimulate speaking, listening, reading and writing is to keep things fresh – that's 'fresh' for the whole school community. But how? Here are two ideas I've seen in my visits to schools.

1. One of the most impressive schools I've ever seen was in the midst of doing a 'whole school text'. In this case it was Shakespeare's *The Tempest*. At every level in the school, the teachers and children were interpreting some or all of the play in their own ways. At nursery and Reception level they were looking at islands and storms. At Year 6 level they were discussing betrayal, obedience, slavery, colonisation, freedom, justice and learning whole speeches. They were talking, reading, writing, doing art work, dance, drama and the pupils were passing on their enthusiasms across the year groups and upwards and downwards. The teachers were working together. This was an ordinary local authority primary school in the inner city.

It struck me that schools could do this in a variety of ways: pick a text that works for all age groups as with *The Tempest*; pick a text that has many texts within it like e.g., *The Greek Myths* or *Myths Across Cultures*; pick an author who writes for different age groups like Michael Morpurgo or Malorie Blackman; pick a country or culture like e.g., The Caribbean, or France or the US and work at all levels on that.

2. Most children's written work goes into exercise books, where they are mostly read by one person (the teacher) and handed back to the child. If we bear in mind that schools have all the potential and facilities to be publishing and performance houses (publishers and theatres and film-makers) we could re-imagine schools as places where children's writing is constantly being found an audience. It is through audience that we discover whether what we write is saying anything interesting. It is also through audience that we have to make an effort to get the surface stuff right: punctuation, spelling and presentation.

So, why don't we make as much effort as possible to circulate children's writing and performance through e.g., blogs (they only take a few minutes to set up and can be regulated in the 'settings'), bulletins, wall magazines, booklets, anthologies, videos, 'cabarets', video shows, poetry slams, writing clubs, parent-child 'family memory' books and so on? This has to be a whole school policy and one that has to be constantly renewed and revitalised, involving parents and carers. It fundamentally changes what we mean by 'marking' a piece of writing.

I've seen it work!

I often post thoughts on education, literature, and current affairs on my blog at: http://michaelrosenblog.blogspot.co.uk

You can also follow my work at: http://www.michaelrosen.co.uk

Lightning Source UK Ltd.
Milton Keynes UK
UKHW01f1837191018
330853UK00001B/323/P